FINANCIAL ACCESS
IN THE
21ST CENTURY

Comptroller of the Currency
Administrator of National Banks

Comptroller of the Currency
Administrator of National Banks

Financial Access in the 21st Century

Proceedings of a Forum

Held on
February 11, 1997
Washington, DC

Foreword

Eugene A. Ludwig
Comptroller of the Currency
Washington, D.C.

Few retail consumer businesses can keep their doors open for long if they fail to attract and retain new customers. In the increasingly competitive financial services marketplace, banks and their nonbank competitors know well that today's overlooked business opportunities may be tomorrow's missed profits and may even threaten their viability.

Thus, I have been puzzled often by why so many of our nation's lower income consumers conduct their financial affairs outside of the traditional banking industry. Is this phenomenon best explained by consumer choice? Weak profit potential? A nonbank edge in lower-income product and service design and delivery? The high cost structure of regulated depositories? Or merely a lack of consumer access to the physical facilities of insured banks and thrifts?

To explore these and related questions, I asked the Consumer Bankers Association last fall to co-sponsor with the OCC an industry forum examining the business case for expanded access to financial services. This publication, "Financial Access in the 21st Century: Proceedings of a Forum," presents the substance of our day long discussion earlier this year among bank and nonbank financial service providers, economists, sociologists, technology and delivery system manufacturers and vendors, consumer representatives, and government officials.

We came together to gain knowledge about the financial service activities of the millions of households across our nation who do not own deposit accounts or otherwise maintain relationships with insured depositories. We came together to share the experiences of banks and nonbanks that have pursued successfully business opportunities with those nonbanked households. And we came together to explore the economic, social, and regulatory barriers that may impede access to financial services by such a large number of American households.

We learned that profitability, in itself, may not be a barrier if providers are willing to be creative in their product design, marketing, and delivery to lower income consumers. We learned that opportunities exist for expanded customer relationships among, not only those who have never had a relationship with a banking institution, but also among those who have recently left the depository fold and those who are only marginally within it. We learned that new technologies are lowering cost structures and spurring new product and delivery system designs that may soon portend greater access to traditional banking institutions. And we recognized that the congressional mandate to make all government payments electronic by 1999 will change, not only how millions of today's unbanked federal payment recipients access their funds, but also the competitive landscape of financial service provision in lower income communities.

The assurance of financial access is vital to the OCC's core mission. This forum is only part of a much broader access-oriented program at the OCC that includes our compliance responsibilities under the Community Reinvestment Act and fair lending laws; our encouragement of national bank involvement in community development activities; and our research, outreach, and advocacy directed at the exploration of new business opportunities among underserved segments of the financial service marketplace.

Expanded access is fundamental to the OCC's mission because it will promote greater consumer choice, a more competitive marketplace, and increased business opportunities for financial service providers. And we know that greater participation in a fuller financial service system brings with it real benefits to households entering the economic mainstream.

Even with the benefit of our forum's discussion, we still do not know nearly as much as we should about the millions of American households, who do not maintain deposit accounts at insured institutions. We need to understand better these households' financial service needs, how they meet those needs today, and how they might meet them tomorrow. I encourage our forum's participants and others to explore these and related access-oriented questions in the months and years ahead. We have made access an ongoing priority at the OCC, and I am particularly pleased that we have recently established the National Access Committee to institutionalize the OCC's commitment to further research and policy development in this area.

We would not have the benefit of this rich volume were it not for the strong support and commitment of the Consumer Bankers Association on this project. Particular thanks are extended to Richard Hartnack, CBA's chairman and the vice-chairman of Union Bank of California, and Joe Belew, CBA's president, for their contributions to the forum discussion and their dedicated work in planning the event with the OCC. Treasury Under Secretary for Domestic Finance John D. Hawke deserves our gratitude for his frank luncheon discussion of the Department's many challenges and exciting opportunities in implementing the congressional EFT '99 mandate. And, finally, I wish to acknowledge the contribution of Ralph DeLeon and Karen Furst of the OCC, who provided essential planning and logistical support.

Mostly, though, I want to thank each of the forum's many participants for their valuable contributions to this most important inquiry. I learned a great deal from our discussion—far more than I ever expected. I am particularly pleased that we are able to share their insights now with a broader audience through the publication of this volume.

Additional copies of this publication can be obtained by sending $15 for each book to Comptroller of the Currency, PO 70004, Chicago, IL 60673-0004. For further information, view our website www.occ.treas.gov/pubs1.htm.

Table of Contents

Welcoming Remarks

EUGENE
LUDWIG,
Comptroller
of the
Currency

We are thrilled to sponsor this forum, "Financial Access in the 21st Century." I think this conference can accomplish a lot of good. I will introduce the forum with three thoughts. One is to emphasize what we do not know. It is remarkable how little we know about the population of the unserved and underserved. Before we determine what can or should be done about this issue, we have to understand the population better and the efforts thoughout the country to serve the people it includes.

Thanks to Professor John Caskey of Swarthmore College and others, we know a little about the unserved group. We know that 12 million households, about 12.5 percent of the population, do not have deposit accounts. In addition, a large, but unknown, number of people are underserved. The unserved represent a third of all minority households; one of four renters; one of six of those under 35 years of age; and 15 percent of the working poor, that is, families earning between $10,000 and $25,000. That population, combined with the underserved, is large, but certainly does not represent the majority of the population of the United States.

Second, I want to mention the possibilities and the tremendous benefits from exploring how we can better serve the unserved and the underserved. I have spoken around the country about the democratization of credit. If you look at that process in some detail, it is enormously exciting.

I refer to this institutionally and personally. President Lincoln, who established the Office of the Comptroller of the Currency, had a strong interest from a young age, when he entered politics, in setting up a national banking system. This was due, in part, to his father's lack of opportunity. His father was a farmer who was never able to succeed at farming. He moved from farm to farm and did not establish a

1

stable household. Several tragedies intervened, including the death of his mother, but I think Lincoln viewed his father's situation in part as lack of opportunity to obtain financial services. So Lincoln was interested from an early age in a national banking system that could spread across the country and provide services.

We have seen for the last 200 years a democratization of financial services. Services once thought impossible or unsafe have become mainstream activities that are now fundamentals of the banking business. Home mortgage lending, for example, was prohibited to national banks as late as the turn of the century. When the first car loan was made by a banker in Illinois, the OCC examiner made him write off the loan, because he believed that was unsafe per se to make a loan on a moving vehicle. But, in fact, during the Great Depression, not only did car loans grow from $20 million to $600 million in volume, but the consumer portfolio performed better than the commercial portfolio.

Indeed, the progenitor of Citicorp entered the retail banking business because the city of New York wanted an alternative to pawn shops, which city officials believed were preying on people. Citicorp had to hire two former pawn shop owners to help them form the retail business. Consumer lending is now the mainstay of Citicorp's business. But it did not happen naturally or easily.

The country has moved beyond that great vision of the democratization of credit to the democratization of services. I believe that herein lies an enormous opportunity, and our focusing on the issues today can provide a basis for furthering that opportunity.

The third thing I wanted to say is, that we do not want to be in the position of implying that "We're the government, we're here to help you." Although government can play a positive role in terms of bringing people together to discuss what can be done, in truth, government can also play a negative role.

Thomas Norton of Western Union told me last night that as a business matter, company executives literally pinpoint the location of Western Union on a map of the United States to ensure that its presence is everywhere. They believe that having a broad geographic spread is the way to do business most sensibly in order to serve the customer. Now, the reason why banks do not follow suit is not a matter of stupidity or venality, but rather of government

policy. For virtually a century, banks have been prohibited from looking at their market rationally when they could, because of unit banking and other branch banking rules and the enormous costs associated with opening branches. So public policy probably impeded the kind of market access that Western Union has been able to provide.

So, although government can play a useful role, it must be judicious about the definition of its role. This conference is useful because before we take action, we ought to know what is happening. In that spirit — a spirit of learning and sharing knowledge before one acts (if one does act) — I am pleased to open today's activities. I will turn this over to Joe Belew, who had the vision, the courage, and the energy to help us convene this group to address these important problems.

JOE BELEW, President, Consumer Bankers Association: The Consumer Bankers Association is delighted to participate in this forum. We enjoyed working with the OCC staff in creating this forum, and I am very excited about it. I plan mostly to listen today, because we have assembled some of the best-informed thinkers in and around the industry that I have seen in a long time.

At the risk of delaying the proceedings, I want to compliment the Comptroller for coming up with this idea in the first place. This is another example of the leadership he has shown. I remember the first time I met you, Gene, in your office. You quickly said that you had a couple of things you needed to do, first, to move forward on CRA and fair lending, and second, to make sure the banking industry was not an anachronism. You have done wonders on both issues and on behalf of our board I compliment you.

We have developed a good formula for today's agenda. First, we will put some facts on the table, so that we are not proceeding from a mythological base. Second, we need to discuss the business climate from both the private and public sectors' perspectives. Third, similar to a Venn diagram, we want to identify the intersections and see what is possible. There is a lot to be learned. As Gene said, this forum is a learning experience to which I am looking forward.

Defining the Market

What market research is being conducted on financial service needs of nonbanked households? What are the findings? Who are the nonbanked and what services do they use? What is their current level of activity? What more needs to be known?

Characterizing the Nonbanked Population
Several participants drew from survey data to characterize the nonbanked population, while others presented findings from focus groups or more anecdotal experience. Based on this information, a variety of hypotheses were presented on why nonbanked households do not use banks and why they use alternative financial institutions and informal financial services.

JOHN CASKEY,
Swarthmore College

I will spend a few minutes reviewing the research that government agencies and others have conducted on defining the unbanked. First, I would have to say that we do not know the percentage of the population that is unbanked. The Yankelovich Monitor database says 6 percent. The Federal Reserve's Survey of Consumer Finances says 13 percent. The Population Survey of Income Dynamics, which focuses on lower-income families, says 22 percent. (All of these measures are weighted to represent percentages of the overall population, not of the particular group surveyed.) So we do not know the exact percentage. The Survey of Consumer Finances' estimate may be a good guess, since it is in the middle of the range.

There is more agreement on who are the unbanked. Everyone agrees that they are primarily low- and moderate-income families, with household incomes of $25,000 and less. They tend to be less well-educated than the overall population; that is, families headed by someone with a high school degree or less. The household head is more likely to be younger than is true in the overall population, say, younger than 35 years old. Household heads over 60 years old are more likely to have bank accounts. The heads of unbanked households tend to be non-white and to rent rather than own their homes. Interestingly, we do not have

3

any information on the breakdown of rural versus urban.

A consensus is emerging from the surveys that address the question of why the unbanked do not use banks. The foremost reason seems to be that they have no financial savings at the end of the pay period. They live from paycheck to paycheck. Banks bundle payment services and savings services, so if people do not need the savings services, they do not use banks. Instead, they buy only the payment services.

The second reason they do not use banks is that they do not like bank fees, particularly account fees. They do not maintain sufficient funds to avoid those fees. People who have low balances in their accounts are inclined to bounce checks and incur bounced check fees. A third major reason is that they want to keep financial records private to avoid government attempts to enforce child support judgments or to evade debt collectors, immigration officials, or taxes. A smaller category of people are merely uncomfortable dealing with banks. Finally, some say that banks will not let them open an account, and I presume that they have a history of bounced checks and outstanding debts.

One myth that I believe is important to correct is the view that people do not use banks because they lack physical access to them, that banks are not located in low-income areas. This may be important in some areas, but not nationally. Plenty of check cashing outlets are located directly across the street from banks, or even in some cases inside the bank, and people still go to the check cashing window.

The unbanked are not synonymous with the customers of check cashing outlets. Many of those customers are unbanked, but many others have bank accounts. The latter use check

TABLE 1
CHARACTERISTICS OF HOUSEHOLDS WITH AND WITHOUT DEPOSIT ACCOUNTS SELECTED AREAS, 1996

	Households without Deposit Accounts		Households with Deposit Accounts	
	Percentage	Number	Percentage	Number
Age:				
a. 18-24	4.6	9	5.9	41
b. 25-34	22.2	43	25.0	174
c. 35-49	32.0	62	32.5	226
d. 50-59	37.6	73	34.2	238
e. 60 or older	3.6	7	2.3	16
Highest education level:				
a. No high school degree	20.2	40	9.4	66
b. High school or GED	44.9	89	38.8	271
c. Vocational/technical school	13.1	26	10.6	74
d. Some college	12.1	24	19.0	133
e. Two-year college degree	4.0	8	8.7	61
f. College degree or more	5.6	11	13.4	94
Annual household income:				
a. Less than $5,000	17.2	31	6.6	44
b. $5,000 to under $10,000	20.6	37	9.1	60
c. $10,000 to under $15,000	22.8	41	17.7	117
d. $15,000 to under $20,000	17.2	31	20.8	138
e. $20,000 to under $25,000	20.0	36	39.1	259
f. Over $25,000	2.2	4	6.6	44
Race or ethnicity:				
a. White	39.8	74	64.0	440
b. Black	49.5	92	27.2	187
c. Hispanic	5.4	10	2.5	17
d. Asian	0.0	0	0.9	6
e. Native American	2.7	5	2.3	16
f. Other	5.4	10	3.1	21

Source: John P. Caskey, "Consumer Financial Services and the Poor," Swarthmore College, Draft paper, October 4, 1996. Collected from a telephone survey in Atlanta, Georgia; Oklahoma City, Oklahoma; and five smaller cities in Eastern Pennsylvania.

TABLE 2
USE OF FINANCIAL SERVICES BY HOUSEHOLDS
WITH OR WITHOUT DEPOSIT ACCOUNTS
SELECTED AREAS, 1996

	Households without Deposit Accounts		Households with Deposit Accounts	
	Percentage Responding Yes	Number Responding Yes	Percentage Responding Yes	Number Responding Yes
Why no deposit account?				
a. Bank account fees too high	23.1	46		
Which fee is the biggest problem?				
1. Monthly account maintenance fee	40.0	18		
2. Check-writing fees	20.0	9		
3. ATM fees	11.1	5		
4. Bounced-check fees	28.9	13		
b. Banks require too much money just to open an account	22.1	44		
c. Don't need account because we have no savings	53.3	106		
d. Not comfortable dealing with banks	17.6	35		
e. No bank has convenient hours or location	8.5	17		
f. Banks won't let us open an account	9.5	19		
g. We want to keep our financial records private	21.6	43		
Where do you usually cash checks?				
a. Bank, savings and loan, or credit union	48.5	96	91.0	636
b. Grocery store	23.2	46	3.4	24
c. Convenience or liquor store	4.5	9	0.6	4
d. Check-cashing outlet	17.2	34	1.0	7
e. At employer	1.5	3	0.4	3
f. Somewhere else	1.5	3	0.9	6
g. Did not cash any checks	3.5	7	2.7	19
Does this place usually charge you a fee for cashing checks?	41.4	77	7.9	53
If you cashed a check this year, did you ever use a check cashing outlet?	45.5	87	13.2	89
If so, about how often?				
a. 1-5 times	45.7	37	69.4	59
b. 6-20 times	33.3	27	23.5	20
c. 21 or more times	21.0	17	7.1	6
How many times did you purchase money orders this past year?				
a. Never	15.8	29	52.2	354
b. 1-10 times	15.3	28	30.2	205
c. 11-30 times	29.5	54	10.2	69
d. 31 or more times	39.3	72	7.4	50

Source: See Table 1.

cashing outlets, because they have so little money in their account that when they get their paycheck, they cannot take it to the bank and cash it immediately. The bank will insist that they deposit it and wait for it to clear. Still other people use check cashing outlets for convenience and are willing to pay for it. They want their cash right away, and the check cashing outlet may be right across the street from where they work.

Where do the unbanked obtain financial services? It is useful to think about four different financial services: check cashing, savings, payments, and credit. The unbanked mainly use banks for cashing checks, even though many banks charge fees. They also use grocery stores and check cashing outlets. Nationally, 10 percent to 20 percent of this population are regular users of check cashing outlets.

Cash is the main form of savings for the unbanked. Other forms are household goods or precious items, such as jewelry. In many low-income communities there are stores that buy and sell gold. For the unbanked, that becomes a form of saving.

About 60 percent to 70 percent of the unbanked purchase 10 or more money orders a year. Check cashers note that many customers cash their checks and purchase a variety of money orders to pay bills, plus one made out to themselves, because they do not want to leave the check cashing outlet with a large amount of cash. They make long-distance payments with money orders or wire transfers. They use utility bill payment services operating at check cashers, grocery stores, and convenience stores.

The unbanked have a large need for consumer credit. Most of them have small financial savings and no financial margin of safety. When bad things happen to them — a job layoff, an illness in the family — they need consumer credit to smooth consumption over time. Many of the unbanked also have bad credit records, which accompanies the lack of financial savings. Very few of the unbanked have

TABLE 3
HOUSEHOLD USES OF CREDIT
SELECTED AREAS, 1996

	Households		
	Percentage answering "Yes"	Number responding to question	Number answering "Yes"
Have a Visa, MasterCard, Discover, or Optima credit card?	48.7	900	438
If so, is it secured?	18.2	424	77
Personal loan from bank or S&L in past year?	8.6	899	77
If so, was most recent loan for less than $700?	20.0	75	15
Personal loan from credit union in past year?	5.1	900	46
If so, was most recent loan for less than $700?	23.3	43	10
Personal loan from finance company in past year?	10.1	899	91
If so, was most recent loan for less than $700?	56.3	87	49
Received payday loan from check cashing outlets in past year?	1.2	900	11
Had "auto title" loan in past year? (Only asked in Georgia)	9.1	187	17
Received pawnshop loan in past year?	5.0	900	45
If so, how often:			
a. 1-3 times	71.1		32
b. 4-10 times	24.4		11
c. 11 or more times	4.4		2
Used rent-to-own in past 2-3 years?	5.4	900	49
If so, did you intend to purchase rented item?	73.5	49	36

Source: See Table 1.

general-use credit cards, although many have store credit cards.

For emergency cash, they find extra work. They also juggle their bill payments, paying the most pressing bills first and delaying others. They approach family, friends, or employers when they need to borrow money. Secondary sources of loans are financial institutions, small loan companies, pawn shops, rent-to-owns, and some check cashing outlets, which offer high-interest payday loans.

CONSTANCE DUNHAM, Office of the Comptroller of the Currency: Households use a variety of formal and informal financial services, including savings, transaction, insurance, investment, and credit services. As a result, no single indicator can summarize fully the degree of household involvement in the formal financial sector. Deposit ownership is one, but only one, indicator of the degree to

which U.S. households are involved in the formal financial sector.

The following charts depict deposit ownership patterns and are based on data from the Federal Reserve's 1992 Survey of Consumer Finances, the most recent data available. The first two charts refer to household ownership of deposit accounts — total balances held in any kind of deposit account (savings, checking, money market, or brokerage accounts) and held with any type of financial institution (such as banks, thrift institutions, credit unions, or brokerage houses). These charts show large differences in the rates of deposit account ownership by households of different income levels, race, and ethnicity.

Chart 1 indicates that substantial portions of low-income households did not own deposit accounts, for example, 30 percent of all households with less than $15,000 in household income. Many other low-income households

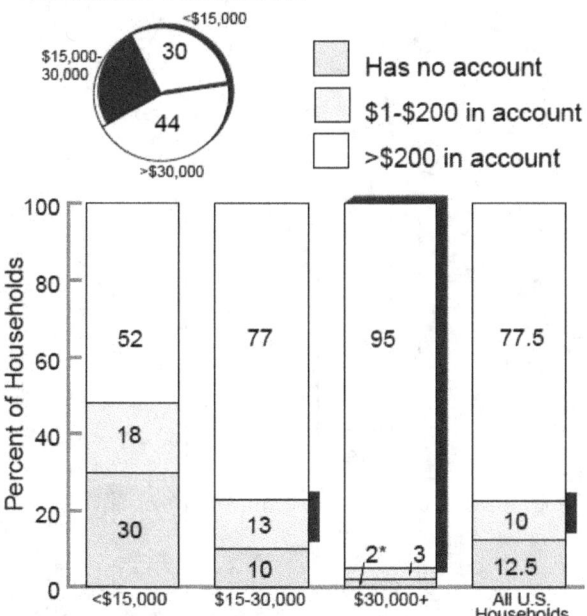

CHART 1
HOUSEHOLD OWNERSHIP OF
DEPOSIT ACCOUNTS, 1992
BY HOUSEHOLD INCOME

* Indicates a sample size less than 30.
Source: Based on data from the Federal Reserve Board, 1992 Survey of Consumer Finances.

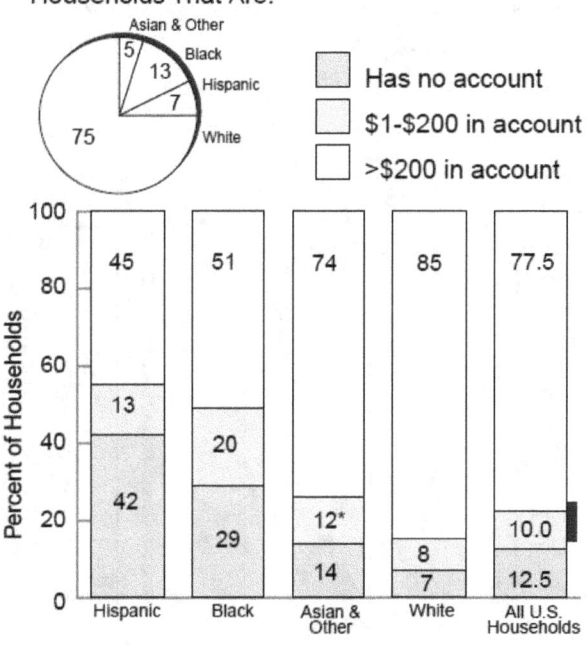

CHART 2
HOUSEHOLD OWNERSHIP OF
DEPOSIT ACCOUNTS, 1992
BY RACE AND ETHNICITY

* Indicates a sample size less than 30.
Source: Based on data from the Federal Reserve Board, 1992 Survey of Consumer Finances.

had deposit accounts with typical balances of $200 or less. Many of these households did not have balances large enough to obtain immediate availability of funds from their deposited paychecks, and some may have cashed their checks at alternative financial institutions, such as check cashing outlets. In contrast, almost all of the households with incomes of more than $30,000 owned deposit accounts with balances exceeding $200.

Chart 2 shows the patterns of deposit ownership for households that differ by race and ethnicity. Again, we see some profound differences. Large portions of Hispanic and black households had no deposit accounts. In contrast, almost all white households owned deposit accounts, and the great majority of these held total balances exceeding $200.

The last two charts refer exclusively to households lacking checking accounts in 1992

and show that the patterns of checking account ownership also vary with income, race, and ethnicity. They also show that over half of all households currently without a checking account had held one in prior years, indicating that, for many, there is no absolute bar to owning a checking account. The data do not reveal why those households stopped using checking accounts. Some may have found that the benefits were not worth the cost. The accounts of others may have been closed because of repeated overdrafts or other misuse. The best we can say is that the data indicate the degree of mismatch between product design and patterns of customer usage.

KENNETH ROSENBLUM, Chase Manhattan Bank: We see a fair amount of diversity in what we call "unbanked potential clients." To give you a sense of this diversity, it was not unusual,

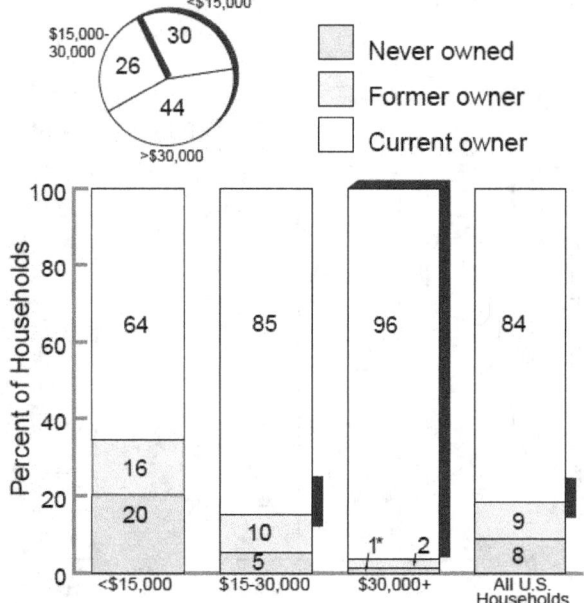

CHART 3
CURRENT AND FORMER HOUSEHOLD OWNERSHIP OF CHECKING ACCOUNTS, 1992 BY HOUSEHOLD INCOME

* Indicates a sample size less than 30.
Source: Based on data from the Federal Reserve Board, 1992 Survey of Consumer Finances.

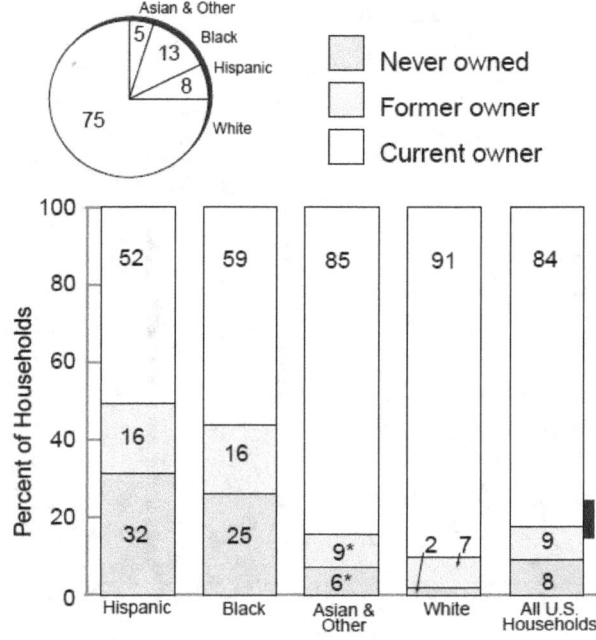

CHART 4
CURRENT AND FORMER HOUSEHOLD OWNERSHIP OF CHECKING ACCOUNTS, 1992 BY RACE AND ETHNICITY

* Indicates a sample size less than 30.
Source: Based on data from the Federal Reserve Board, 1992 Survey of Consumer Finances.

though not the norm, to sit in focus groups and hear customers of check cashers talk about their mutual fund accounts.

We also give credence to the cultural norms related to why people remain unbanked. Some people elect to cash their checks to preserve their privacy and prerogatives. They may believe that what they earn belongs to them, and they want to keep that a secret. For example, some may cash their check, take the overtime pay to spend as they like, and make available the rest of the paycheck, the base pay, to the family unit.

Another dramatic finding of our research is that check cashers are far superior to banks in terms of the days and hours they are open for business and their ease of access. Many banks close at three o'clock in the afternoon, while most people leave work much later. People are willing to pay for the convenience. We are spending much time and attention on improving access for our customers.

The research also revealed that many people prefer using a check casher rather than a bank because they believe that they are being judged by the bank teller. The bank teller's request for the customer's identification and scrutiny of it made people uncomfortable. They were seeking a nonjudgmental interaction. In fact, they expressed a distinct preference for using automation, such as ATMs, wherever possible to avoid being judged.

The final issue that emerged is personal security. People want to be comfortable that their transaction is not observed, and they are not exposed or put at risk when they leave the premises. That has become a major consideration in assessing our current channels and developing new ones, whether they be standard branches, our checks-to-cash club program, or supermarket banks in low- and moderate-income areas.

I would estimate about 7 percent of the residents in the New York metropolitan area marketplace are unbanked. Our research, which includes both focus groups and quantitative analysis, corroborates many of the same characteristics mentioned already in terms of income, ethnicity, etc.

PAMELA FLAHERTY, Citicorp: Citicorp's perspective comes not from conducting research on the unbanked per se, but as a bank looking at marketing to low- and moderate-income consumers. We found great diversity within this population.

For example, we found that Hispanics were much less likely to be tied into the formal financial network than were certain other ethnic groups. We also found large differences among groups in attitudes, ages, and incomes. So combining all these people into one group may not be a good way to discover what it is that they really need.

(The discussion of nonbanked households by Paul Hammond of Yankelovich Partners has been withdrawn because the firm is not confident that the underlying data represent a reliable portrait of the nonbanked, and the firm plans to develop more reliable data.)

MICHAEL SHERRADEN, Washington University: I am going to comment briefly on the poorest population, which has been my major focus. I do not have a lot of systematic research about how people save. Most of my work has focused on the difference that having assets makes in people's lives, which is a slightly different question from how people save. We have conducted some in-depth interviews in St. Louis with public welfare recipients and public housing tenants, who were put in small group samples of five and ten in different parts of the city. I would like to give you some observations about their financial lives based on these in-depth studies.

The poorest people have few economic options. They are living on the edge. A minimal number have a relationship with a formal financial institution. In the past some of them had a checking or savings account, but usually they do not have accounts when they are receiving public assistance or living in public housing. As Carol Stack found in the 1970s, this population still relies on friendship. The risk is pooled because they rely on one another. If they run out of money, they borrow from friends or relatives. As Professor Townsend found, there is a lot of "reduction of consumption," which means that in a crisis, their consumption level goes down until they can re-establish a little bit of income.

ROBERT FRIEDMAN, Corporation for Enterprise Development: Most of my experience over the last 20 years has been looking at how low-income people move forward economically.

9

I do not have definitive data. My information is anecdotal and impressionistic, but it is important in that it focuses on the behavior of people who are moving forward.

Saving is not encouraged by the culture. Saving is not easy, especially in low-income communities, where few incentives to save exist. So I find it is useful to look at programs that give some support to saving. My experience is mostly with the microenterprise, or self-employment, movement in this country; with savings groups; with individual development accounts (IDAs); and with asset-building.

People complain that they do not have a place to save. Frequently, loans made to a participant were dissipated to friends and family members whose claims in a financial crisis can be overwhelming. We also found a desire by these persons to repair their credit histories, and to establish relationships with banks. They often take that as a point of honor, even if they have to pay taxes as a result.

The poor are often offered lesser incentives to save than the non-poor. I had an experience 30 years ago, when I was lined up behind several middle-aged African-American women who were depositing money into a Christmas club account. I remember (not understanding information and transaction costs) asking the teller what interest was paid on these accounts. She said, "Oh, no. This is a service we provide. We don't pay interest."

We found a lot of reinvestment in small businesses. We were concerned that people were drawing out less income from their businesses than they could afford. We asked why and were told, "Don't you see, I'm reinvesting in the business so that I can grow it, so that tomorrow I can get more back." We found, particularly among low-income microentrepreneurs, including welfare entrepreneurs, that asset build-ups were much larger than we expected, both in the business and personally. Two-and-a-half years after certain welfare recipients had started businesses, they had accumulated about $5,000 in net business assets and $9,000 in gross personal assets that they did not have before.

LISA MENSAH, Ford Foundation: Some excellent research on the unbanked population has been presented today. I think that foundations should support more of this research.

I would like to reiterate some of the evidence that Robert Friedman has shared about asset building in the microenterprise field and to cite some of the research that Professor Sherraden has provided about saving among poor populations. I do not think that poor peoples' latent interest in saving can be underestimated. This interest is not endorsed in this country.

Immigrants and Foreign Remittances

Foreign remittances are an important payments service for many immigrant households. Participants discussed the implications of foreign remittances for understanding the financial service needs of nonbanked households.

MARTIN LIEBERMAN, Community Currency Exchange Association of Illinois: The Hispanic community studied by Professor Townsend, is extremely unique. Hispanics traditionally have very strong family ties. Even though the concept of a "mattress bank" may apply in some of the other poor communities, Hispanics send money back home.

The vast majority of Hispanics are here for a short period of time, to make money and send it to their families. Often the money to open a business comes from Mexico. Conversely, we sell money orders to Hispanics regularly and a great portion of the money returns to Mexico via Western Union.

So the Hispanics' relationship to banks is unique. They do not believe that they are going to be here long. They do not want to establish a relationship. They come to the United States to support their families abroad.

ROBERT TOWNSEND, University of Chicago: Although some Hispanics may not have formal relationships with banks because they send a lot of money to their homes outside of the U.S., the average residency of Hispanics in our study was 16 years. This indicates that many Hispanics also have a long-term strategy of establishing residency and citizenship in the U.S.

We also have "nonresident" Hispanics who run businesses from outside of Little Village. This subgroup is more upper-income, more fluent in English, and more connected with others outside the Hispanic community.

EDWARD FURASH, Furash Associates: We should remember Harry Truman's saying:

"The only thing new in the world is the history you don't know." We cannot ignore history when we talk about the unbanked, because the problem of reaching and serving them has a long history.

For example, this discussion of foreign remittances makes it seem as if it were almost a brand new problem. But foreign remittances were a substantial activity in the 19th century, beginning with the Chinese immigration. Thousands of men from China came here to work on the railroads and to send money back to their families. That did not prevent the Chinese community, over time, from becoming a major force in the world of commerce in some parts of this country. The Chinese accomplished that by pooling funds in the community. So a concern that foreign remittances might harm an immigrant's ability to build a life here is not historically based.

The other waves of immigrants who came from 1890 to 1923, until passage of the immigration restriction acts, also sent large amounts of money home. The fact that many immigrants come here today to support their families at home is not a new phenomenon. Nor should it be used to criticize whether or not immigrants also start businesses here. They came here to support their relatives in their native lands or to bring them here. That is what America is all about.

Savings and Insurance for Short-Term Emergencies and Long-Term Goals

Participants discussed whether there is untapped demand for saving by low-income households; the purposes for their saving; and the implications for the design of new vehicles to respond to those needs, to stabilize their economic positions, and to support asset accumulation for their economic advancement.

MICHAEL SHERRADEN, University of Washington: My primary interest has been savings. The unbanked do not constitute a population that typically thinks about savings. Low-income people will tell you that they do not have enough money to save. Even the word "savings" means something different to them, so more ethnographic work must be done. To very poor welfare populations, the word "savings" means, foremost, efficient consumption. You

save if you use coupons or buy at secondhand stores.

Savings, as it is understood by welfare recipients is almost always short-term savings. For welfare mothers it often means saving for a child's winter coat, for something needed for school, or for money for a school trip. Those considerations are important to welfare families.

In those households there is almost no discussion or hope for long-term savings. The welfare rules have discouraged long-term asset accumulation. I am pleased to say that welfare rules limiting assets are beginning to be eased in the 1990s. More than 40 states now have raised their asset limits. I believe that changes

> ...if the instruments are appropriate, there is a demand for savings in a very low-income population.

have taken place largely because of the recognition of the need for low-income households to be able to accumulate assets.

What would facilitate savings in this population? Some may believe that savings in this population may not be possible. I do not agree with that view, although my belief is not supported by much empirical evidence. We must conduct more demonstration programs with different financial instruments.

I refer to the work of Marguerite Robinson, whose paper is included in the forum background materials. She interviewed low-income Indonesians about desirable savings vehicles. The People's Bank of Indonesia (Bank Rakyat Indonesia, or BRI) developed six or eight savings instruments for different purposes. The population showed by their responses that an extraordinary latent demand for savings existed in Indonesia. I think the BRI now has 12 million savings accounts: about six savings accounts for every credit account. This is convincing evidence that, if the instruments are appropriate, there is a demand for savings in a very low-income population.

I have several observations from an experiment with electronic benefit transfers (EBT) for welfare recipients in a St. Louis neighborhood. EBT will be available for that population and represents a huge opportunity to bring financial services, not only benefit transfers, but also a range of financial services, to this population, resulting possibly in greater savings.

Anecdotal evidence from both those working in the EBT system and participants revealed that participants tended to have some money left at the end of the month. Most of the welfare population does not even reach the end of the month before having to rely on food pantries. The EBT money was kept a bit separate and not as available to the demands of friends and family. So a population that typically has no money left at the end of the month had a little bit left. This provides some evidence to support the development of EBT systems that structure, and perhaps even give an incentive for, savings as a segregated part of the account.

Individual development accounts (IDAs), which involve matched savings, provide large incentives for savings at low-income levels. The matching amounts can come from either public or private sources. We can also be creative about incentives associated with savings that provide some fun, because there is little money in these households for any kind of entertainment. Perhaps we can provide incentives that allow people to have movie tickets or a coupon to eat out at a local restaurant.

About nine out of 10 welfare recipients we interviewed said that they would save if someone matched their savings one-to-one. Although we do not have much empirical evidence for this, the Corporation for Enterprise Development is starting an IDA demonstration program at 10 sites and will conduct a long-term evaluation of how much people can save in IDAs.

Besides the surveys and neighborhood studies, we also need more demonstrations of particular instruments or programs that facilitate savings and to conduct carefully-controlled studies on their effects.

ELISABETH RHYNE, U.S. Agency for International Development: Coming from the international perspective, I am very familiar with Marguerite Robinson's experience in Indonesia. Initially, a large unbanked population there did not save in banks. The instruments that BRI developed to meet that need were connected closely to transaction services; they were simple savings products with various liquidity features.

I am struck in listening to this discussion by the difference between long-term savings services and liquidity management services. Yankelovich data indicate that people generally want to save to protect themselves against emergencies, for an annual vacation, and for children's futures. Those desires will motivate people regardless of their cash flow. But John Caskey spoke of the need for liquidity management services.

Traditional bank accounts marry those two types of services, so the longer term savings (i.e., required cash balances) provide a cushion for liquidity management. The banking system is structured so that if no cushion exists, your check will bounce or you will have to pay fees and penalties.

So it seems to me that offering savings services that appeal to longer term needs somewhat separately from those that meet liquidity management issues will be a key to developing a service structured for this population. This service would appeal to the undeniable desire of people to save for the longer term, which in turn would support the liquidity management needs. The two functions would be provided, but would not be so closely tied together that liquidity management fluctuations negate longer-term savings.

ROBERT TOWNSEND, University of Chicago: Our survey in Little Village, Chicago, shows that nonbanked people are interested in better ways to cope with emergencies. One motive for savings, for example, is to buffer emergencies and shortfalls. That was one of the most important distinctions between the populations of banked versus nonbanked.

In the Indonesia experiment, savings accounts multiplied rather dramatically after BRI introduced new savings instruments. A key feature of those instruments was that the depositor could withdraw the money at any time. For example, the bank allowed people to withdraw savings on demand for holidays, such as Ramadan, an important Islamic event. With this assurance, savings would accumulate, decline during Ramadan, and accumulate again. A product was offered to meet seasonal needs as well as emergencies. In contrast, many nonprofit organizations are promoting a type of mechanistic savings. They assume that the poor do not know how to save, that they have to be taught to save, and that they should save regularly and accumulate funds.

What products do we have in this country to enable low-income communities to cope with risk? Savings is one way to meet the high risk they often face, especially if it has the right costs and attributes. Insurance is another method. For example, consumer finance companies could offer consumer loans that require customers to buy life, disability, unemployment, and other insurance. That mechanism, once in place, could be expanded, so that the insurance costing a higher premium could provide larger amounts of compensation and be adapted for other circumstances. There are institutions that currently offer insurance in small amounts to the low- and moderate-income population. We know how to do that. Can banks do it?

HAL NIERNBERGER, HALsystem, Inc.: The core issue here is that no receptacle exists for savings for the poor. Basically, their only vehicle is the instrument known as the "mattress bank." Savings accounts, even credit union accounts, are designed for people who are already in the system. The basis for saving must be a vehicle that offers transaction services as well as the capability of laying away funds for future investment or savings, not formal savings, but a replacement for the mattress.

DONALD NEUSTADT, Ace Cash Express: We try to facilitate transactions for our customers and they come back to us and say, "We would love to be able to save through you." I am not necessarily saying that such households will begin a long-term savings program for the next generation, but these persons do recognize that they have a responsibility to put aside some funds. Based on the findings of focus group research, I believe that many people would be interested in a service that would allow them to save a portion of the check they are cashing, as long as they have reasonable access to it.

KATHARINE MCKEE, Self-Help: In reading the background materials, in listening to conversations, and in becoming acquainted with Professor Townsend's research, I was impressed that there seems to be more of a discontinuity in savings instruments than in the lending area. Relatively few savings options are avail-

Is the mattress bank myth or reality?

able to the less-well-off than are offered to higher-income customers. More products have been designed that meet credit needs than savings needs. I would like to ask Professor Townsend what kind of evidence he has about the degree of satisfaction or dissatisfaction with the mattress bank option. How did survey respondents characterize their savings options?

ROBERT TOWNSEND, University of Chicago: Unfortunately, the answers to that await us. Our survey was factual, finding out about the savings experience of the household currently and in the past, how households coped with hard times, and how they got businesses started. We did not venture much into the territory of opinions. We plan to ask this in focus groups.

RICHARD HARTNACK, Union Bank of California: It is unclear to me whether, in fact, there are barriers to savings that we are presupposing in this conversation. Is the mattress bank myth or reality? Do we really have poor people living in neighborhoods with households full of cash? I do not think so.

You must recognize that we have many different populations here, from older people who have no desire to start a business or save money, to urban and rural persons, and everything else. When my bank put together what I would describe as a "barrierless" savings account — no minimum balance, no fees, no nothing, just put money in regularly — the product appealed to only about 30 percent of the households in the check cashing segment.

So is the presupposed desire to save universal? Even if only some of these persons want to save, what are the barriers to savings? Can we overcome them by offering the savings account, which is an incredibly simple product, in another environment? Do people not save because they do not want to come to a bank? Could we offer savings accounts through check cashers or liquor stores or other outlets?

KATHARINE MCKEE, Self-Help: I can offer one example to answer your question, Mr. Hartnack. Durham, North Carolina, has a rapidly growing Hispanic population. In the last month, the newspaper has carried an account every three or four days of break-ins by a violent bunch of thugs into houses inhabited by several Hispanic families or an extended family. As much as $1,000 was taken in some of these robberies, which are now being called "home invasions." I was startled by that figure and by the level of savings that that represents for people who have not been long-settled in our area.

PAMELA FLAHERTY, Citicorp: Many persons in the mortgage business, in formal financial institutions, have now recognized informal group savings as a legitimate way for persons to produce down payments. The informal groups with which I am most familiar in New York are called sou-sous. West Indian and Caribbean persons meet in these groups to save money. When a group accumulates the first targeted amount of money, say $3,000, one member is given those funds to use as a down payment. The members continue saving until everyone has received funds for their down payments, which they make through formal institutions. This is an example of a linkage between the informal and formal sectors.

EDWARD FURASH, Furash Associates: The problem of financing the underbanked may not be question of less available funding, but rather of more choices of where to put money. Earlier in our nation's history, when the constraints on the underbanked were at least as great as today, few banks were involved. Immigrants and underprivileged groups had few savings and investment vehicles and were forced to rely on their own community to pool funds and to borrow.

Because of deregulation, consumers have more places to put their money. They can choose to keep it at home, in the community, in a bank, or in a money mutual fund to earn a higher yield. Consumers wishing to protect their own interests are trying to manage unanticipated consequences. They may believe that it is not as secure to put their money into a pool (where they may or may not be repaid by neighbors they may not trust) as merely to put it into a high-rate bank certificate of deposit.

Although pooling vehicles still exist, they are not working as they did in the past. Many of the people who could use them have safer investment alternatives; local business investments are more complex than they used to be; and their communities may be drawn in differ-

ent directions rather than to a central core of funding each other.

The diminution of prejudice has acted against the formation of self-help groups. Self-help groups in the last wave of immigration basically were fostered by prejudice. As a result new residents to the United States were afraid that bank employees were not going to give them any money, and that they would have to look elsewhere. Now it is easier to get money, but the process is not necessarily better. I believe that for community-based solutions, one should look at communal self help. Bank-community partnerships are crucial in the absence of self-help funds pooling, because a bank cannot have the force of the community.

What More Needs To Be Known?

JOHN CASKEY, Swarthmore College: What additional information do we need to understand further the problems of the unbanked and underbanked? All the current surveys are imperfect. A large-scale household survey targeted at low-income people should be conducted, as well as in-depth neighborhood studies. We do not know much about rural-urban differences or about differences by specific demographic groups. Our current data are limited in terms of sample size. For example, some surveys have a sample size of a little over 200 unbanked people, which is too small for assessing specific demographic categories.

On the credit side, we do not know much about variations in state regulations. States that have restrictive usury laws have fewer pawn shops, small loan companies, or payday loan businesses. We do not know who obtains credit in states without those institutional sources of high-cost, high-risk credit. We also know very little about how other countries deliver financial services to low-income persons with small savings.

Finally, there is the issue of the cost of delivering payment services to the unbanked. Those who cash their checks consistently at a check cashing outlet will pay more for payment services than those who maintain a bank account and obtain services through the bank. There are good reasons for that. If a customer has $1,000 in the bank and cashes a check, the bank is not really taking the risk, since it has the $1,000 balance as collateral. The customer who maintains a savings account lowers the bank's cost of providing payments services.

So if we are interested in lowering the cost of financial services to low-income consumers, we should encourage them to build financial savings. Here we need more research, since we do not know how to increase the savings of low-income households. For example, we do not know which of the many consumer education programs work well.

Formal and Informal Financial Services

Robert Townsend, professor of economics at the University of Chicago, presented the following address to forum participants based upon his ongoing research in a low- to moderate-income Chicago neighborhood. He emphasized the importance of understanding household behavior better, the causes of community development, and financial activity in low-income communities to develop more effective financial sector innovations and government policy.

ROBERT TOWNSEND, University of Chicago

I do not think there is much dispute that the higher one's income is, the more likely one is to use checking and savings accounts and other financial services. We should, however, focus, not only on income levels, but also on the growth of income and its fluctuations. Our country's economic development has been aided in no small part because of our strong financial infrastructure. But if not everyone participates in the financial sector, we will have growth with inequality, with some people lacking access to educational, occupational, and other opportunities that enable them to advance.

Growth with inequality has engendered a variety of efforts to improve access. In the public sector, the federal government has responded with the Community Reinvestment Act (CRA) and the Equal Credit Opportunity Act (ECOA). In the private sector, nonprofit organizations carry out much community-level activity, as do banks. Even beyond CRA requirements, many banks and other financial service organizations now view the middle- and low-income market as an opportunity to carry out profitable activities.

Beneath the surface descriptions of low- and moderate-income neighborhoods are more fundamental issues of supply, demand, and economic barriers. To be more effective, governments, banks, and nonprofit organizations should define clearly their understanding of people's behavior and subject that understanding to facts. This would provide a more useful framework for designing and evaluating financial sector innovations, government policy, and notions of community development and social welfare.

This approach differs from the measures typically used to evaluate community development and social welfare, such as the number of customers, the volume of credit, and the percentage of credit denials. Neither those measures, nor simple correlations linking income and financial service use, are the kinds of key facts upon which we should focus. We will not improve matters by trying to undo those correlations, but rather by going beneath their surface to better understand household welfare and the causes of community development. The measures that are the most important are based on a good understanding of the needs of households and small businesses, and the actual situation in which they operate.

Along with two of my colleagues at the University of Chicago, Richard Taub and Marta Tienda, I have tried to do that by studying the

> A policy that encourages saving
> could be important for
> long-run economic growth and
> increased equality.

needs of households and small businesses in Little Village, also known as South Lawndale, a low- to middle-income neighborhood in Chicago. We interviewed 327 Hispanic households and 235 Hispanic businesses, as well as a large number of Koreans in that neighborhood. Our effort is complemented by the work of John Caskey, who has obtained detailed information, which we have not, about currency exchanges (check cashing outlets), consumer finance institutions, and other financial institutions that operate in similar neighborhoods.

Little Village has banks lining the streets: commercial banks, savings and loans, and other financial service institutions, all of which compete heavily with one another. One bank recently renamed itself Banco Popular in an attempt to increase its client base. Yet there is a belief that none of these banks has succeeded in penetrating the neighborhood.

Nonprofit organizations include ACCION International, which opened in Little Village a couple of years ago to extend its services to low-income Hispanics. ACCION carried out a marketing survey in advance to determine whether to enter that marketplace. About 96 percent of the households responding to this survey said that they would appreciate having a microcredit lender in the neighborhood, indicating the existence of a large latent demand for small loans. ACCION has gotten off to a relatively slow start in Little Village, however. Its group lending approach never took hold, although it has made loans to individuals.

Liquidity Constraints

In our research we used a conceptual model of people's behavior. If shown to be consistent with the facts, the model can underlie useful government policies and financial innovations. It presupposes that while the economy grows, people discover potentially profitable investments, such as new occupations or small businesses. Since these investments require money, low-income people without access to sufficient sources of credit cannot invest in these opportunities. Instead, they remain low-skilled, low-wage workers.

Conversely, other people, by dint of inheritance or good fortune, have sufficient funds to invest in high-profit opportunities. On average, they earn high profits, which they reinvest. Their companies grow, their sons and daughters have access to money, which they reinvest, and so on. That process does not continue forever, however, as wages eventually rise and workers can slowly save their way out of liquidity constraints. Over time, their income growth approaches overall economic growth, leading eventually to a reduction of inequality.

We collected data to test whether this model of economic growth provides an accurate picture of Little Village. First, we found that business start-ups in Little Village are profitable. For every dollar spent in start-up costs, a business earns on average about 70 cents per year in profits. The risk of business failure exists, with about 62 of the 235 businesses surveyed replying that they were in danger of failing over the business's lifetime. Even adjusting for that risk factor, however, 70 cents to the dollar suggests that profitable business opportunities exist and businesses can grow in Little Village.

Among the households who took concrete

steps to start businesses, but did not eventually do so, 50 percent of our survey respondents cited lack of credit and loan rejections as their principal problem. That information is consistent with our model. Moreover, of the businesses that did start up in Little Village, 58 percent began entirely with the owner's own savings, that is, without any loans at all. Others obtained help from sources in the informal financial sector, such as friends and relatives. Business start-ups were rarely financed with loans from banks.

The dollar magnitude of the start-up costs of businesses was strikingly different for different ethnic groups. The following are ranked from lowest to highest in terms of business start-up costs: Hispanic residents of Little Village, Hispanics who are not residents of Little Village, Asian-Arabs, and whites. Differences between the Korean and Hispanic communities account for part of the discrepancy in start-up costs. Korean business owners reported they finance their larger business start-up costs with greater personal savings and borrow from other Koreans through business partnerships.

The implications of this framework are that:

• Policymakers should realize that a policy that encourages savings could be important for long-run economic growth and increased equality. We should explore the barriers to savings to determine whether we can increase the facility and use of savings instruments throughout the population.

• In our study we found that networks in the informal sector often financed business entry in some population groups. Perhaps we should consider how to lessen the liquidity constraints for members of other population groups that contain fewer networks. We could encourage the formation of more networks. We also could investigate whether and how formal financial institutions can substitute partly for the lack of such networks. But first, we need to understand better what these networks accomplish and how.

• Most importantly, we need improved intermediation, the flow of funds from savers to borrowers. We want to encourage savings and to use those savings for credit. But the real challenge is how to create more inter-

mediation in the community, so that those who have funds and choose not to invest directly can, through intermediaries, lend the funds to those who face limited access or constraints.

Thus, a key issue relates to liquidity constraints: the ability of some, but not others, to get financing for education, occupational choice, or small business formation. When credit is limited, savings becomes important. However, rather than discuss the relative merits of credit and savings, I want to stress the importance of improved financial intermediation that should guide both financial innovations and public policy.

Risk Allocation

Now consider other elements of the economic growth model. For example, if higher-income households have greater access to the financial sector than lower-income households, we should expect overall economic growth to increase, with growing inequality.

All households face a choice of whether to enter risky occupations (or invest in education, small businesses, etc.) or to stay with "sure-thing" occupations, which tend to have low and fairly stable wages. Staying with "sure thing" occupations reduces risk, but also limits the accumulation of assets. Households can reduce risk by obtaining services from the formal financial sector, even though they may have to incur certain costs to gain access. They may, for example, obtain a conventional insurance policy. Or, they may receive "implicit insurance" by obtaining a loan with flexible repayment terms, such as postponed payment options, or the possibility of extending maturities to avoid formal default.

Both insurance and flexible loan arrangements enable households to allocate better the risks from financial setbacks to which they are exposed. By sharing, or reallocating, these risks, their incomes are more stable. They are better able to invest in high-risk, high-yield occupations and businesses. Their higher average incomes allow them to save more, which they can then invest in high-yield activities, and their incomes grow faster still.

In contrast, many households with limited funds may be unable to obtain formal financial sector services. Without the ability to share or reallocate risk, such households are forced to be financially conservative. They tend to choose low-risk, low-gain strategies. When they suffer economic setbacks, they generally reduce consumption because they have no other way to meet shortfalls.

Households that accumulate savings have a buffer to withstand economic crises, something to draw on when they face financial setbacks. Households with more savings tend to be less conservative financially. They are more likely to invest in high-risk, high-yield activities. Higher average incomes allow them to save still more and invest their savings in high-yielding investments, contributing further to income and consumption.

The possession of savings also means that the household may not need the formal financial sector for insurance services, either those provided by conventional insurance policies or implicitly by flexible loan terms. In effect, households can obtain insurance from their personal savings.

We tested this behavioral model to see if it applies to Little Village. We asked households whether they had experienced a financial setback in the last five years. Fully two-thirds answered that they had experienced serious financial difficulties during that time, due most often to unemployment, sickness, and the death of relatives (see table 4).

We asked households what they would do in a *hypothetical* situation of financial stress. More than half (139) said they would go to a bank and try to get credit, whereas 133 said they would use savings. So banks are on the minds of these households: they are aware of banks' presence and the possibility of using them. (In contrast, the businesses that we surveyed in Little Village were not eager to borrow from banks.)

However, *in practice*, these households do not use banks much. The single most common practice cited for getting by in hard times (36 percent of respondents) was to use personal savings (see table 5). Only 12 percent answered that they borrowed from banks, whereas about 32 percent of the households said they received gifts and loans from relatives and 28 percent received help from friends. About 33 percent deferred payments on previously incurred loans, most of which came from the informal sector.

Only 50 percent of the households surveyed had savings accounts and 21 percent had checking accounts at banks. These and other households who use banking services tended to be richer, more fluent in English, and more connected to others outside the neighborhood. Households that use banks in financial stress situations benefit because they do not have to reduce their consumption as much as those without such arrangements. Households that reported using informal financial services tended to have lower incomes, to be less proficient in English, and less connected to others outside the neighborhood. They also were less likely to own a home or have a home mortgage loan. These results show a classic stratification of household characteristics in Little Village. Many households find themselves in a real bind in hard times and often experience difficult periods.

The policy implications of households' inability to reallocate risk follow:

• Risk is very high for low-income households.

TABLE 4
PRINCIPAL SOURCES OF FINANCIAL DIFFICULTIES AMONG HOUSEHOLDS
LITTLE VILLAGE NEIGHBORHOOD, CHICAGO, 1994-1995

Problems	Households	
	Number	Percentage
Death or illness of relatives	127	38.8
Unemployment or unusually low income	163	49.8
Increase in living expenses/dependents	125	38.2
Total households citing at least one problem	210	64.2

Note: Because multiple responses are considered, sum of responses is greater than total households responding.
Source: Philip Bond and Robert Townsend, "Formal and Informal Financing in a Chicago Ethnic Neighborhood," Federal Reserve Bank of Chicago, *Economic Perspectives*, July/August 1996.

It is not uncommon for them to have to decrease consumption when they suffer financial stress. When policymakers consider social welfare issues, therefore, they should focus, not only on increasing the level of income, but also on improving security against *fluctuations* in income.

- In practice, we do not find that households (or businesses) use banks much for borrowing or for deferring debt. So it seems that the formal financial sector is not playing much of a role in reallocating risk. This suggests that we consider implicit insurance services, or perhaps even explicit insurance policies, for these low- and moderate-income households. Insurance could either be commingled with credit instruments or provided as a separate service.

- Formal financial sector savings are used as a buffer by many Little Village households. Policymakers should therefore emphasize savings as an important financial instrument. But we need to understand better the costs associated with having access to savings and checking accounts for low-income, non-English speaking households.

- Households in the informal sector appear to cope better with risk through the use of flexible-term loans, recip-

rocal gift giving, and so on. Our survey has not documented exactly how such flexibility was accomplished. We need to hold focus group meetings within the neighborhood to gather this data and to see if methods exist that the formal sector might possibly imitate.

TABLE 5
HOUSEHOLD RESPONSES TO FINANCIAL DIFFICULTIES
LITTLE VILLAGE NEIGHBORHOOD, CHICAGO, 1994-1995

Response	Households	
	Number	Percentage
Financial response (new source)		
Borrowed from banks or individuals*	25	11.8
Gifts or other assistance from relatives*	68	32.1
Borrowed from friends*	59	27.8
Gifts or assistance from friends*	28	13.2
Borrowed from ethnic association*	17	8.0
Used credit cards	5	2.4
Transferred payments	28	13.2
Received money/food from community organization	1	0.5
Financial response (existing assets)		
Used cash or household savings*	76	35.8
Sold assets*	17	8.0
Delayed or failed to pay debts*	66	33.1
Labor response		
Works harder/increased hours*	88	41.5
Got other job to tide over*	46	21.7
Put other family members to work*	25	11.8
Consumption response		
Reduced household consumption expenditures*	97	45.8
Other		
Received nonmonetary help from relatives	2	0.9
Somebody else will pay	1	0.5
Other	20	9.4
None, because it did not cause economic problems	14	6.6
Migration	1	0.5

*Responses explicitly mentioned as an option in the questionnaire.
Notes: Total number of households responding = 212.
Because multiple responses are considered, sum of responses is greater than total households responding.
Source: See table 4.

Thus, a second key issue involves the reallocation of risk. Banks allocate risk-bearing, but it is costly for many people to use bank services. Some observers have concluded that we should focus on lowering those costs. However, much risk allocation is already occurring in the informal sector in ways that may be better suited to the needs of many households and small businesses.

This implies that policymakers should focus on improving access to savings as a method of insurance or on improving access to appropriately designed, formal-sector insurance services. These are potentially important ways for banking organizations to respond better to the financial needs of low- and moderate-income households.

Information, Incentives, and Financial Service Design

A model of economic behavior and growth might make the assumption that the poor have less access to credit. One plausible scenario assumes that, compared with others, the poor may need a larger loan to invest in education, a new occupation, or a small business because they have few assets of their own. If they obtain a loan, they must repay a larger amount of principal and interest relative to their expected earnings.

This could make the prospect of borrowing less attractive to the poor than to more financially independent households. The poor would face less of an economic incentive to borrow and work hard, because much of their labor would be devoted to repaying the loan. A lower expected payoff, coupled with less work effort, could increase the probability of failure. I am not putting this in pejorative terms. It is only that the poor will tend to find it less economical to earn a return that exceeds their loan repayments.

Lender monitoring costs may exacerbate this situation. If there are fixed monitoring costs per borrower, they will be relatively high for small loans. This gives banks less incentive to make the small loans that poor households tend to borrow.

The model is sensitive to the exact nature of private information incentives. For example, another scenario could presume that the poor work hard to survive and that capital is complementary to labor, so that the marginal product of capital to the poor is higher than to the rich. This would imply that the poor would have greater access to capital than the rich.

In our conceptual model, however, we will assume that the poor have limited access to credit. This means that they are stuck in low-risk, low-yield, underfinanced occupations. In the short run, the economy experiences growth with inequality. In the long run, as the economy accumulates capital, interest rates would fall. This would lower the size of loan repayments, which would allow the poor to benefit more from the fruit of their efforts. This, in turn, would increase their economic incentive to work harder, earn more money net of loan repayments, save more, and become somewhat wealthier.

The poor may be able to improve their situation by creating their own groups. If they are better able than outsiders to monitor each other's labor efforts, they may have a better way to share risk internally without adverse disincentives. Under certain conditions, it may be economic for formal financial institutions to lend to a group rather than to the individual members. In actual practice, we might see this not as a formal group but as an implicit group; that is, one person with access to the formal sector would relend to his or her poor relatives. We have not been able to collect data on this, however.

Our survey of Little Village provides evidence that the poor have less access to credit than others. We also have evidence of networks and groups that vary by ethnicity. Examples reveal family members working together in a business; people forming partnerships by pooling credit and other resources to go into business; and strong networks of co-ethnic suppliers. The networks are stronger among those who have lower incomes, less English proficiency, and less connection to others outside the neighborhood.

The networks are very real. Policymakers, bankers, and nonprofit representatives often think that a government agency, bank, or nonprofit organization is the only game in town, but this is not true. There is a lively Hispanic informal sector with its own arrangements among family, friends, and suppliers. The Koreans have another version that consists of many more non-family professional business partnerships.

Lest I leave you with the notion that informal groups offer a miracle cure, I want to emphasize again that when ACCION International went into Little Village to promote microlending, group lending never began despite the presence of these networks.

The policy implications of these data indicate that:

- We need to understand better the incentive structures of financial services.

- We need to understand better the conditions for effective group lending. Although group lending may work, it should not be viewed as a panacea. We must consider the possibilities of internal insurance, monitoring, and contract enforcement among potential groups.

- Policymakers and banks could consider providing formal loans to informal groups, using identifiable groups as intermediaries. In the Korean community, for example, one can identify rotating credit associations. Instead of lending only to individuals, banks might also consider lending to this kind of informal financial intermediary. This seems to be the thrust of the recent financial development community investment corporations and the Community Development Financial Institutions (CDFI) Fund that was recently created by law and is beginning to lend.

Lenders incur costs of developing information in screening loan applicants and monitoring loans. If these costs tend to screen out the poor, some observers conclude that we need to lower costs to increase their access by the poor. But informal sector information networks may be more effective than formal sector efforts. Group lending arrangements may be effective ways for borrowers to obtain funds from formal financial institutions. Some persons may obtain credit or insurance from institutions and serve as intermediaries to others who are not directly linked. Although we have not measured them, these indirect connections to the formal sector also may offer avenues to increase access.

In conclusion, policymakers, bankers, and nonprofit representatives may need to adopt innovative solutions to increase access to the formal financial sector. At this forum, I have heard two discussions of how check cashing outlets, which service those who apparently are not bank customers, are linked to banks, either vis-a-vis credit or check clearing operations. So perhaps my dichotomy between the formal and informal sector is overdone. Nevertheless, we need to draw the entire picture of the informal and formal sectors before we decide that a radically underserved population exists.

My major conclusion is that we should not examine simple correlations between income and credit volume to assess social welfare, introduce financial innovation, or develop government policy. Rather, we must try to develop a realistic picture of the processes in these communities. We should then base our notions of social welfare, financial innovation, and potential policy change on our understanding of those processes.

Identifying Barriers to Serving the Nonbanked

What are the impediments and business challenges to reaching nonbanked households?

SEAMUS McMAHON, First Manhattan Consulting Group

Perceived and Actual Barriers to Serving the Nonbanked

When discussing financial institution barriers for banks to reach the "underbanked," bear in mind that serving these marketplaces does not mean serving only one segment; they are not only immigrants, nor only minority ethnicities. None of the potential impediments discussed here will cover all of those segments.

Banks face three potential impediments to serving the underbanked: the profitability of the services; materiality, that is, the extent of this business opportunity; and the appropriate "branding" or positioning of the services that banks would provide.

Surprisingly, profitability is almost certainly not an issue. The margins that banks could enjoy on smaller accounts are probably not a challenge to keeping them out of this business. In fact our databases on behavioral characteristics of consumers — we are a consulting firm that works closely with banks — show little or no correlation between the income or wealth of current bank customers and profitability. The reason is that low- and moderate-income customers are equally apt to pay fees and may have only modest servicing requirements.

Indeed, banks have discovered that it is possible to construct a low-cost liquidity account that enables payments against low deposit balances. This sort of account would entail approximately $100 a year in cost, and it is plausible that banks will receive more than that in revenues. So profitability per se does not seem to be a real issue.

Realistic opportunities also exist to cross-sell streamlined loans and insurance products, if banks develop a relationship with unbanked or underbanked consumers. The banking system may not create those loans or insurance products, but banks could serve as an outlet through which third parties could distribute them. So we would reject the notion that profitability is an insurmountable barrier.

A more challenging barrier is whether banks will see this opportunity as too small on a sheer

> Banks face three potential
> impediments to serving the
> underbanked...
> Surprisingly, profitability is almost
> certainly not an issue.

revenue basis compared with other business opportunities. For example, assume that the total national after-tax profits from payments and loans to these 10-to-12 million households could reach the $500 million range for the entire industry, based on the balance sizes and fee structures that we envision. Although that is not a small amount, it represents a small fraction of total banking industry profits, and, in fact, equates to the after-tax profits of the twentieth or twenty-fifth largest bank in the U.S.

However, this business opportunity could grow if banks consider, not only the unbanked, but also people who are marginally banked. These customers typically have small accounts at banks and believe that they are being underserved. Marginally banked customers are some banks' most profitable customers; they can generate $300 or $400 a year in overdraft fees. So this opportunity could be one that banks reach out for — and may be forced to reach for, because current fee sources, such as overdraft fees, are probably unsustainable over time.

I personally think that the biggest impediment to banks explicitly targeting low-income customers will be branding or product positioning. Many banks now target middle- and upper-income customers to compete with what they believe to be their greatest competitors, which are mutual funds, financial advisors, and stock brokers.

In advertising statements, we hear more and more about "the quality of the relationships." Many bank executives we talk to are concerned about their ability to appeal publicly to lower-income customers without clouding the "upscale" image they are trying to establish. Conversely, our own surveys indicate that many lower-income customers believe that there is an unattractive, judgmental aspect to doing business with a bank. The solution to eliminating that impression is unclear. It may be as subtle and as pervasive as a bank's own advertising.

Thus, we see solutions to these potential impediments, with some easier to attain than others. We think that profitability is manageable through a combination of electronics, reduced labor, and customer training. The materiality, or size of business opportunity, looks relatively small today, but could grow dramatically if banks develop appropriate instruments and products for a much larger group than merely the unbanked. And finally, some banks will likely choose to enter this business nationally under one or more distinct brands. So none of these problems is insurmountable.

ELISABETH RHYNE, U.S. Agency for International Development: I would like to report on the findings of a conference that the U.S. Agency for International Development (USAID) sponsored in November 1996. It brought together about 25 commercial banks from around the world that were engaged in microfinance, which includes lending to microenterprises, or very small businesses. Although this is not exactly the same situation, I think that the findings of that conference apply to this discussion.

First, commercial banks that successfully reached the informal sector did so through separate outlets, not through their main branches. This enabled them to establish a separate image — which relates to the branding issue — and a completely different cost structure from their regular branches.

Secondly, they created a workforce that could reach this customer base — a staff who could relate to the customer, such as people who come from the same communities. This issue was probably the most difficult one for the banks to solve.

Thirdly, there was a need for high productivity among the microfinance staff that exceeded that expected in mainstream banking operations. Because of the small size of transactions, the labor-intensity per transaction was very high, so incentives for high productivity became a crucial issue. The reward of increased pay for improved performance, contrary to normal bank operations, was opposed by the unions representing the other bank employees.

Finally, the internal corporate culture had to change. Employees at all levels had to begin to see this population as a viable, legitimate market. This required a major educational effort within the bank for all employees.

Standardizing or Customizing Financial Delivery Channels

Participants debated whether standard bank branches, or innovative or customized delivery systems, are preferable for providing services to the nonbanked.

STEPHEN BROBECK, Consumer Federation of America: The marketplace may largely be meeting the current demands of the bankless. These demands appear to be quick access to cash (through check cashing and small loans), payments of utility and other bills by money orders, and perhaps convenient location. But the bankless have needs beyond those demands, including access to savings instruments, encouragement to save and not to borrow for discretionary spending, relatively inexpensive services, secure banking, and protection against theft. At present, only traditional banking institutions — commercial banks, savings and loans, and credit unions — can meet those needs.

I would like to comment briefly on barriers to servicing the bankless by traditional banking institutions, which are related to both the characteristics of the bankless and to the characteristic behavior and perceptions of the banking institutions. The bankless may lack income or sufficient motivations to save. They may not be aware of the generally higher cost of using alternative financial services. Some lack skills in using some banking services, particularly checking accounts.

Banking institutions tend to have inconvenient locations or times. Despite surveys show-

ing that these inconveniences are not a major barrier to serving this sector, Consumer Federation of America conducted research about a year ago in Oakland California and found that large low- and moderate-income residential areas contain no banking institutions. Even if residents wanted to patronize those institutions, they would find it highly inconvenient to do so. Other barriers include the relatively high minimums to open deposit accounts and avoid fees, and the refusal by most banking institutions to cash checks and make funds available immediately if there are no funds in an account. Finally, neither bank employers or most of their customers welcome the bankless in their branches, nor do most institutions have customer contact personnel that speak Spanish or Asian languages.

It is not clear which of those barriers are the most important. I suspect they vary for different subgroups of the bankless. This kind of analysis with so many different factors is very complicated. We may be better able to figure out how to serve these groups effectively, if we can identify successful institutions and learn why they are successful.

DAVID JOHNSON, Corus Bankshares: Although we have talked about how the unbanked population is not exactly a homogeneous one, we have been talking about banks as though they are homogeneous, which they are not. Different banks have different missions, different capabilities, and different abilities to offer new technology. For example, our bank is a $2 billion bank in Chicago, which makes us about the 200th largest bank in the country. We are a niche bank with only 12 locations. Our strategy is not to open more locations for any community, whether a private banking, low-income, or middle-income community. Other banks have different kinds of missions.

Banks do operate in lower income areas; to say otherwise is a fallacy. In such areas there are different types of banks, just as there are different types of other institutions, and other kinds of consumers. Neither consumers nor the financial institutions that serve them constitute a homogeneous group.

> The internal corporate culture had to change.

MARTIN LIEBERMAN, Community Currency Exchange Association of Illinois: My view is that the community seems to be well served. I also question the suggestion that there are not enough banks in the community. That depends on the community. There are enough banks. It is just that people do not require bank services, or they perceive that they do not require the services.

The difference between check cashers and banks is basically a difference in attitude. Check cashers are locally owned businesses, whether a check cashing outlet, a liquor store, or another establishment. The check casher staff speak the same language as the person cashing a check, have a first-person relationship with the customer, fill out the forms, work with the person — whereas it is perceived that the bank staff will not, whether or not that is true. This perception may vary somewhat with the specific bank, the specific person, and the specific teller's instructions for processing transactions, but the perception exists.

RICHARD JUAREZ, MAAC Project: I head a nonprofit organization in an inner-city area. Whereas most communities have a 40,000-square-foot supermarket, we have 10,000 to 20,000-square-foot markets. Whereas most communities have super drugstores, we have little pharmacies. Whereas most communities have a 15,000 square-foot Blockbuster video store, we have the 1,000-square-foot Joe's Video. Whereas other communities buy general goods at Kmart and Wal-Mart, we have 99-cent stores. And whereas most communities have banks, in the area in which I work, there is not a bank for a mile and a half. We have a population of 40,000 to 50,000 and one bank, the Bank of America is located there. Union Bank of California is just outside the area. We do not have banks. We have check cashing stores.

I serve on a bank board and have been listening to this discussion from that perspective. But it's entirely different when I step back and don my neighborhood hat. Then this entire discussion about whether those communities should have alternative services is outrageous. It hardly matters whether those services are check cashing as an alternative bank, or the 1,000-square-foot video store instead of the Blockbuster, when the banks really do not want to serve them. The banks are figuring out how

to link with the check cashers, who can assume their burden, so that the banks do not have to go out there and do it.

Western Union takes an alternative approach. It makes a point to serve the entire world, not only the nation and not only my neighborhood. The check cashers have been striving to get in there and serve. Why are the banks not doing the same? The real estate agents go door to door. The insurance agents go door to door, or they mail out their information. Grocery stores send me a flyer every single week, whether I shop there or not. If you want the customer, you have to get the customer. The banks have people with MBAs and a lot of business experience. Banks know how to get customers and how to market.

The issue is one of making the commitment to serve the clients and not only a certain segment of the clients, and the need to change the way the service is marketed. For example, auto salesmen have learned that when they are dealing with an Asian or Mexican family, they have to sell to the family, not only to the person. The product must be different.

In banking a lot of focus has been placed on loans to underserved communities, but there has been little discussion of other kinds of services. In the housing industry, we have changed the way we provide affordable housing to inner-city communities by altering the lending system. We have not changed our thinking in that area, and that needs to be done.

Also there is some question about whether banks would make a profit when providing an intensive level of service to underserved communities. But the underserved comprise only 10 percent of the population, and banks are not making a profit in all areas. Or maybe it should be considered in terms of a long-term effort. If banks are serious about moving to electronic banking, they will have to show some customers first how to write a check and use the ATM.

DONALD HAMMOND, U.S. Department of the Treasury: I wanted to follow up on a comment made by Stephen Brobeck that the needs of the consumer could be met only by an established banking organization. The financial services currently being used in the low-income neighborhood tend not to come from a traditional banking institution, but rather from alternative service providers. Why, if you project toward the future, do you look exclusively to the commercial banking system to provide services that are already being furnished to some extent by alternative financial providers?

STEPHEN BROBECK, Consumer Federation of America: I said that today only traditional banking institutions would meet the important financial services needs of the bankless. That was merely an observation. Frankly, I have not made up my mind about what kind of mix we need. This is why I suggested that we need more research on institutions that have met these needs most successfully.

RICHARD HARTNACK, Union Bank of California: I want to challenge a comment about banks not making a commitment to serve clients in a low-income community. Eight years ago, as a result of a CRA agreement, our bank put a full-line branch in a very low-income community. It has not been successful and not for lack of trying. We tried very hard but have been unable to make it economically successful. Short of using flammable liquids, it is about the fastest way I have found to lose money.

The branch will probably stay there, because it is established under an agreement, and it is an interesting place in which to learn. In all respects it is a traditional bank branch in terms of size, location, facilities, and everything else, except it is in a very poor community, and the economics do not work. Using that platform is not a way to make money.

There is an obvious barrier. If you take all the deposits in all the banks in that community and put them into one office, the branch still would not make money. The aggregate amount of money that is predisposed to go to banks in that community is not sufficient to make money in a traditional bank setting. Banks are good at dealing with money that is predisposed to go to banks. But banks are perhaps not as good at being salespeople for changing culture, changing habits, or changing attitudes toward privacy.

RICHARD JUAREZ, MAAC Project: I suggest that it is a matter of marketing. If the traditional banking approach to serving these communities is not working in that bank, you may need a different approach, using education, personal interaction, and language. There is a movement toward putting mini-banks in grocery stores. Perhaps the bank building is not

the answer. Maybe banks need to go to where the people are rather than expecting that the people are going to find the bank.

RICHARD HARTNACK, Union Bank of California: We certainly have tried everything we can think of. We did not operate the branch for eight years just for the fun of it. We have tried everything within our range of knowledge and capability. The community told us that establishing a traditional branch was the answer at the time of our CRA agreement. So I show it as an example that the opening of a traditional branch in a poor community does not necessarily solve the problem.

We have tried everything to market our services. We have used churches, seminars, knocking on doors, and massive advertising campaigns. The fact is that if we had 100 percent of the market, we would not make money there.

EDWARD FURASH, Furash Associates: I cannot help be impressed by this conversation's focus on the current and the conventional, when this forum's focus is on the issues of the 21st century. I am reminded of the intense arguments after World War II about whether people on public welfare should be allowed to have refrigerators. The answer at that time was "No — as long as the iceman still comes." What happened was that the iceman stopped coming and people had to have a refrigerator as a necessity of life.

Access to financial services in the 21st century is similar. The entire U.S. population must adjust to new methods of obtaining financial services. The old methods will no longer be in use. So new technology must be accessible to all because the financial service iceman is not going to come anymore.

All the traditional methods of delivery, such as the branch or ATMs, have problems, because of a fundamental change in the economics of financial services. Deposits are not worth anything anymore, and consumers do not like paying for transaction services. The reason deposits are less valuable is not that we happen to have low interest rates right now. It is because the traditional way banks made profits — taking deposits, making loans, and living on the spread — is disappearing and has been for 15 years. This business may continue for perhaps another 15 years.

This is because the securities market dominates financial intermediation in the United States today — and will in the 21st century. The prices of deposits or funds are not set by banks. They are set by the money market mutual funds and others in the market. The price of loans is not set by banks, but by the securities markets through securitization.

The traditional technique of subsidizing savers or borrowers by controlling rates disappeared when Regulation Q expired. Deregulation basically drove deposits from the banking system. For 15 years, the banking system has been trying to reduce the cost of traditional delivery methods, because banks can no longer produce deposits at a total cost that enables them to compete against prices in the securities markets.

This is a serious problem as it relates to access to financial services in the 21st century for the unbanked. Regardless of the degree to which we may think the unbanked have been disadvantaged, they actually have been, for a long time, the beneficiaries of a subsidized deposit system. The subsidy is disappearing because deposits are not worth much and the cost to gather them is high. The costs that the unbanked are paying check cashers is probably a better reflection of the pure cost of transaction services than what they pay in a bank. Banks are still subsidizing.

What are the choices? This is a social, not a financial issue. Is the only choice to tax banks by saying they have to deliver in a traditional manner? We have tried that one, and people

> If you phrase tomorrow's needs in terms of how we deliver things today, we always return to subsidizing the unbanked, and I do not think we can afford to do that.

do not necessarily come to the CRA store. Or are we going to guarantee access through government subsidy, such as issuing bank stamps, as we do food stamps?

Market competition has a better answer. Critics may not like the prices charged the unbanked to serve them, but they are better served because entrepreneurs and bankers see an opportunity there. We must encourage participation by providers who can do all the

chores, fill out the forms, and provide financial attention, and can get paid for doing them. If the price is too high, others will emerge.

The 21st century will present a radically different financial service environment for the unbanked. Checks will not be an issue, nor will supermarket branches or kiosks. The critical solution is deciding how the unbanked can make transactions that allow them to participate fully in society, buy the necessities of life and, hopefully, be able to set aside money. Ultimately, this will require an electronic distribution system, if they are to have economic opportunity.

As we look at the 21st century, our real goal is to ensure that, first, we create prosperity in this country. That is what banking is about. And second, that everyone has an opportunity to interact with the financial system and to get the most they can for their money in doing so. If you phrase it that way, there are many new players that will enter the scene with new ways to do it. But if you phrase tomorrow's needs in terms of how we deliver things today, we always return to subsidizing the unbanked, and I do not think we can afford to do that.

Financial Service Design and Customer Service
Participants discussed barriers that can arise from financial service design and customer delivery.

THOMAS NORTON, Western Union: I think that any commitment to service low-asset, low-income households requires a "mechanistic" commitment. Many of these consumers are confused and intimidated by forms. It is common in many of Western Union's agent partners for a clerk, or even the owner, to help the customer fill out a simple name and address form. This can take a lot of time.

Many consumers do not have conventional identification, such as driver's licenses, military identification cards, or birth certificates. Now, it is certainly acceptable for the Manhattan elite to not have a driver's license, but for somebody trying to apply for a loan or cash a check, the absence of one requires a bank employee to make a big decision.

In our experience, many of these consumers are transient. They might move within the metropolitan area or from Houston to Florida to do roofing every summer. This is intimidating

30

for a bank that lends to these folks and sees the initial payment coupons returned two weeks after they were mailed.

Because these households are hard to reach by mail, you must have mechanisms in place to take their payments in person during the hours when they are available, often after conventional banking hours. So one has to make a series of logistical commitments to these consumers.

JIM MEADOWS, Citizens National Bank: Our bank delivers traditional banking services. We tend to make money at it, and our profits are, compared with our peers, very high. Our income statement is characterized by high levels of net interest income, high levels of noninterest income, and a low and stable funding base.

Whatever successes we have had in serving the low-income market has resulted from our willingness to do so. We are a one-unit bank, in one location, and our customer base is primarily ethnic and low- to moderate-income. It was a market that was given to us, and so we began with the premise that it would be our primary focus. This is not a niche of our business, but our primary focus. So everything we do is geared toward finding ways to identify the needs of those customers, to price rationally, and to serve that business.

We have high costs because we have lots of customers in our bank and lots of employees talking to customers. We have close relationships with the public schools. We tend to reach more people through their children in schools than we do any other place. We do not have a lot of trouble getting traffic in our lobby, it is thrust upon us at nine o'clock every morning. We have high security costs in our bank, not so much for threat of robbery but for directing traffic. We have a lot going on — not a lot of deposits, but a lot of activity.

EUGENE LUDWIG, Office of the Comptroller of the Currency: Professor Townsend gave us a picture of Little Village, where the street was lined with banks. And one fact that seemed to emerge from several of his stories is that savings could be a boon to economic development.

If there are banks in Little Village that offer savings vehicles, and the population would benefit from saving, why do people not use the banks? It is not as if customers have to go 100 blocks to reach a bank branch, or an eight-hour drive, as was once required on the Navajo reservation. The banks are right there. I would be interested to learn why people are not going to the bank offices.

DONALD NEUSTADT, Ace Cash Express: We operate in 29 states and have a fairly wide population base. Many of our customers are "trial rejecters," who previously had a relationship with a bank. They have had access to some kind of a loan or credit facility. Perhaps a lender terminated that relationship because of abuse. Or perhaps the customer chose to terminate it, because they had a negative experience, and went elsewhere.

Consumers are aware of banks and have tried them. But, for whatever reason, the customer relationship did not work out and the customers are less likely to return and try to reestablish a banking relationship. We have conducted focus groups with customers that show that they trust us, like us, and have a different view of us than they may have of financial institutions that closed their accounts.

We hire our employees from our customer base, so they understand our customers and cater to them. I am not criticizing bank hiring practices, but banks typically hire people who are more able to cater to the customer segment that banks want. I think that this is a significant part of the difference between the type of customer service we offer to our customer base versus what banks offer.

MARVIN MORRIS, In-Person Payments: In Main Street America people are allowed to make bill payments at our locations. We have taken this service, not only to check cashers, but also to pharmacies, hardware stores, and beauty shops. Customers go to a trusted person in the community, who could be the pharmacist or the person who runs the hardware store. They find it appropriate to discuss financial questions and services with them.

RICHARD HARTNACK, Union Bank of California: We have conducted numerous consumer interviews with our check cashing clients to find out why they do not use the bank. In our case it is very dramatic. The bank and the check cashing window are in the same building, in the same lobby, and use the same parking lot. The choice is obvious and they choose the nonbank solution. The reasons are all over the map and include having had an unsatisfactory experience with banking. These people are well described by the term, "trial rejecter," and their negative experience can relate to their own personal discipline, to literacy, or to a variety of things.

For some the issue is privacy. Some people, for a variety of reasons, want to keep their financial circumstances as opaque as possible. Illegal immigrants have no desire to develop a relationship with a bank, which they see as a quasi-governmental body. This is particularly true for people who come from countries where banks were part of a government that was oppressive or provided an element of risk. Others have had legal difficulties with a spouse or someone who is suing them and do not want to have money in bank accounts. A number of people use both bank and check cashing services. They have two lives: their wage-earning life and another aspect that they do not want people to know about.

EDWARD FURASH, Furash Associates: Providers exist today who deal with the risk of providing financial services to the unbanked. When a check casher decides to cash a check, he takes on risk for which he is paid. Banks that handle check cashing more conservatively are merely stating they will not compete at that high a risk.

Perhaps the pool could be enlarged of those who will compete on the risk of widening financial service access through insurance, cross-subsidization through pooling, or cross-guarantees — preferably on a private-sector basis. This might give the less-served and the unserved the level of service that they need to ensure their access in the system in the next century.

Partnerships Between Banks and Nonbanks in Serving the Nonbanked
Participants discussed the merits of partnerships between banks and nonbanks as strategies for overcoming barriers to reaching the nonbanked populations.

MARTIN LIEBERMAN, Community Currency Exchange Association of Illinois: I encourage those at this forum to think, not only of

how your own particular industries operate, but also how to align yourselves with those of us who are now, and have long been, serving the community. For example, the first food stamp I distributed was on the very day they were introduced — and at that point I had been in business for years.

There are definite advantages to a partnership between check cashers and banks. We, in the check cashing industry, believe that we do not compete with banks, and that a partnership is a logical conclusion. Check cashers have space that is less costly than bank lobby space and have generally lower operating costs. They work longer hours and are open more days in a week than are banks. Check cashers could lend to banks their location, staff, and understanding of the marketplace. Our discussion today reveals that a glaring flaw in the banking system is its lack of understanding of the motivation of nonbanked persons.

Check cashers, however, need access to the federal banking system. The government at all levels is comfortable working with banks. Banks are insured, sophisticated, and have the ears of the legislators. Promising new products that have a good chance for success, both within the community and in the political arena, all seem to point to a partnership between the banking world and either state-run check cashing associations or individual check cashing companies.

STEPHEN BROBECK, Consumer Federation of America: Our research on branch closings in Oakland revealed that virtually all of the branches that were closed in a 15-year period had assets under $20 million. Most branches with assets over $20 million remained open, suggesting that profitability may be related to the size of a branch's asset base. This raises the question of whether banking institutions will find it profitable to serve the unbanked without charging high prices. Although they can lower costs by downsizing their branches and putting them in supermarkets, that might only reduce the break-even point to a $15 million asset base. Many communities will be unable to support even that lower asset base.

To serve those communities we may have to turn to institutions that have very low costs, such as the U.S. Postal Service. Postal banks in Europe meet many of the needs of low-income households. If banks could accept this option, not only would more of those needs be met, but also banks would operate under less pressure to meet the financial services needs of low-income and unbanked populations.

The second way to meet those needs involves using nonprofit institutions. The banking services they provide would be subsidized basically by foundations, their for-profit funders, the government, and the people who volunteer or work in these nonprofits for low wages.

LISA MENSAH, Ford Foundation: We should also consider the wealth of institutions in the communities that we are discussing. Rather than talking about people as if they were disassociated persons, we should consider the mediating institutions that are not represented here or in our discussion. Churches, local civic organizations, local community development corporations, and other smaller institutions do mediate in people's lives and help them to navigate through the emergencies and the stresses.

These institutions, which have been concerned traditionally with low-income populations, would be helpful allies. They would operate as strategic mediators or providers of information, which are important roles when attempting to reach a population that is unbanked.

KATHARINE MCKEE, Self-Help: Nonprofit community development financial institutions (CDFIs) constitute potential partners of banks and nonbanks. Self-Help is the largest of the 500 nonprofit CDFIs across the country, with about $100 million in assets. Although our sector is relatively small in size, we work largely with the customers that we have been discussing today.

To date, there have been quite a few partnerships on the lending side between banks and CDFIs. We want to work with banks and nonbanks to see if technology can help us better serve our core customers, the small businesses and home buyers, who will be left out by a credit scoring world. I also see potential for joint work in providing our customers with access to new financial products for savings and investment. They may be more receptive to those products as customers of CDFIs. We would benefit to the extent that we help families build assets and stabilize their economic situation. This relationship could help our bank or nonbank partners acquire, at lower cost, customers who are receptive to their products.

Many CDFIs would like to offer to our customers an account similar to a Union Bank of California account. Perhaps kiosks or other kinds of simple technology could be located in CDFIs, which could help increase customer acceptance of the new technology. Partnerships could also be forged between CDFIs and the offerers of the new individual development accounts, now being broadly tested, which provide incentives for savings by low-income households through matched contributions. CDFIs could help their customers find productive investment uses for the savings, such as starting a microbusiness or purchasing a home.

Many CDFI depository institutions could also benefit from technological help in their transformation from a manual-labor, volunteer-dependent structure, which is untenable.

LARRY STOUT, Financial Management Services, U.S. Department of the Treasury: One important issue I would like to address is how technology can be used to make significant links between traditional and nontraditional financial service providers. I work for the part of Treasury that issues some 850 million payments a year primarily to benefit recipients (Social Security, Supplemental Security Income, Veterans Administration, civil service retirees). In our research of that population, we found that about 15 percent remain unbanked. We found that they did not like a checking account or overdraft charges, nor did they believe they needed a checking account.

To identify a product that might better serve the needs of that population, we built a pilot program in Texas, which linked the traditional bank providers with ATMs and point-of-sale terminals at the grocery stores where those persons cashed their checks and bought money orders. We developed a product that they liked, would use, and for which they would pay a reasonable price. Although some people have an aversion to technology, we must face the fact that technology is with us now and will continue to facilitate the linkage between traditional and nontraditional providers.

I believe that electronic payment will provide our constituents with the greater safety, convenience, and protection that accompanies having an accessible place to deposit money. Benefit recipients are 21 times more likely to have a problem if we issue checks than if we deposit their payments in accounts electronically. Problems that arise from electronic payment can be resolved in two to four days, whereas it takes at least two weeks to solve a problem about a check. Since it costs Treasury 43 cents to issue a check and only two cents to make an electronic payment, we can solve a problem in a manner that combines good government with providing better service.

Effect of Government Policies on Serving the Nonbanked

Participants discussed how banking regulations, government policies regarding receipt of public welfare benefits, and federal tax policy incentives for household savings and investments may serve as barriers to attracting and serving nonbanked households.

JOHN CASKEY, Swarthmore College: Gene Ludwig mentioned regulatory barriers earlier. Regulatory barriers may currently prevent banks trying to serve low-income populations from developing small offices that may house a different type of staff and culture and may not offer loans or a full range of services. Other regulatory barriers could also keep banks from teaming up with check cashers, which could take deposits and provide banking services to this population, perhaps as an agent for the bank.

We have talked about brand name identification. Political problems may arise for any bank that tries to tailor its services to different population groups. A bank that served a high-income area might have leather chairs and private banking loan officers. Already, some bank ads offer private banking services to customers with at least $5 million in assets. Middle-class banking would tend to resemble large supermarkets. Finally, lower-income banking would offer a different kind of branch in low-income areas and minimum service, based on fee-for-service. The fee structure would be different in each place. Banks would be asked why they do not give everyone exactly the same thing — that is a political reality that banks must face.

We must consider building an inclusive investment system.

SEAMUS MCMAHON, First Manhattan Consulting Group: I understand the potential problems that exist for banks, but the facts are different. About 30 percent of the currently banked population pay about $100 or $120 a year in revenues to banks, but cause banks to incur costs of $150 to $400 per year. These customers are extremely unprofitable to banks and the banking industry will have to develop a lower-cost solution for them. It is plausible that the same solutions that would provide for low-cost outlets, high-productivity labor, or different branding, could apply to multiple segments of income. People would not be differentiated solely by income, but by what they are willing or able to spend on banking services.

PAMELA FLAHERTY, Citicorp: Banks are under pressure regarding their services to all customer groups. This is not just an issue of providing services to certain segments versus others. The banking industry is changing. The way we conduct our business, where we are headed, and how we serve different customers is a subject of intense debate. Bankers all over America are trying to understand the research on how to serve customers in a changing world where the economics are very different.

The economics are changing for all customers. Many assume that all the profitability issues for banks are linked to income characteristics, but I do not think that the evidence supports this.

JULIA JOHNSON, Banc One Corporation: I have a question for John Caskey. Do needs-based tests for eligibility for public benefits serve as a disincentive for asset accumulation?

JOHN CASKEY, Swarthmore College: Michael Sherraden, who is here, is the expert on that. I would say no and yes. Yes, it does after you reach a certain asset level. Many states declare people who have more than $1,000 in financial savings as ineligible for welfare. That is clearly a disincentive. You do not want to accumulate more than that amount if you are on welfare or expect that you will go on welfare. But we could still encourage people to accumulate and maintain $300 in their savings account, which would lower their cost of payment services. In most states, that would not be an impediment to receiving benefits.

ROBERT FRIEDMAN, Corporation for Enterprise Development: One significant barrier to savings are the welfare regulations that stipulate that persons can have only $1,000 in assets before they lose eligibility for welfare and access to Medicaid. Three other barriers transcend and surround the kind of barriers we have been discussing: consumption orientation, lack of hope and expectation, and lack of tax incentives for savings.

The first is cultural, particularly as it applies to poor communities. For at least 50 years, assistance to these communities has been oriented toward income maintenance, consumption, and debt. We have believed that we need to sustain consumption in low-income communities. Our income maintenance system is built upon that. As a result we have honored savings in the breach, not in practice. I think that is as true in the development community as it is in the institutional structure. We have tended to emphasize low-income housing and only recently focused on low-income home ownership. We concentrated on microenterprise loan funds and only now have shifted emphasis to savings incentives and structure to provide an equity base in low-income communities. An income maintenance structure can maintain consumption, but it does not provide ladders out of poverty. We need to develop an inclusive investment system.

The second set of barriers involves hope and expectation. If you do not expect that you can find a way out of poverty, you do not try. We know that kids who get pregnant early and kids who commit crimes may do so because they do not have hope. Michael Sherraden notes that "assets are hope in concrete form." We have seen that even with small-scale savings clubs and IDAs, that when a low-income person buys a house, it raises the expectations of the entire community, who may think, "Oh, if she can do it, then I can do it." We need to do much more to develop those escape routes from poverty and those success stories.

Thirdly, we use tax policy as an incentive for the non-poor and wealthy to save. But this policy does not offer the same incentives to the poor. We subsidize, or (if you prefer) incentivize, the saving of the non-poor and largely the wealthy, through the tax system: the home mortgage deduction, preferential capital gains treatment, pension fund exclusion, individual retirement accounts (IRAs), and Keoghs, etc. Any new trend in savings incentives offered by the government is through continued use of the tax system — through the expansion of IRAs, 401(k)s, and medical savings accounts, etc. Again, none of these systems provides equivalent incentives to the poor. We must consider building an inclusive investment system.

Mandatory EFT '99

JOHN HAWKE, Under Secretary for Domestic Finance, U.S. Department of the Treasury

I would like to begin by describing the process of preparing paper-based Social Security benefit checks. The process begins very early in the month, after the Social Security checks have been sent out for the previous month. Each payment check is inserted, along with any flyers, into an envelope, which is then closed. Piles of these sealed envelopes are stacked onto carts, which are then rolled into a section of the building containing cart after cart of numbered and carefully arranged Social Security checks.

Later in the month, the Social Security Administration provides information about the people who have recently died or become ineligible for Social Security. Somebody goes back to these stacks of checks, finds the checks for those people, pulls them out, and withdraws those checks from the process. Then the remaining checks are picked up by the Postal Service, which puts them in the mail system. One has only to spend a few hours watching that process to get a dramatic view of how labor- and paper-intensive the paper-based payments process is for the 30 or 40 percent of Social Security payments that are not made electronically.

All that will soon change. The capable staff at the Financial Management Service (FMS) who process those paper-based payments will have to find other work within the next couple of years. Last year, Congress passed a law with a deceptively simple mandate: all federal payments made after January 1, 1999 shall be made by electronic funds transfer.

Often referred to as "EFT '99," this act covers every payment that the government makes (including vendor, salary, benefit, and retirement payments), except for tax refunds. The statute gives the Secretary of the Treasury the authority to develop standards for granting waivers for classes of recipients or instruments for hardship or other circumstances.

That waiver authority will have to be used selectively or the benefits of the electronic program could be undermined.

Each recipient of those payments is required to designate one or more financial institutions or other authorized agents to which payment shall be made. The statute does not say when or how this is to be accomplished. That is the decision of FMS and the Treasury Department. But, by January 1, 1999, we know that recipients will have to give instructions about where to send their electronic payments.

The Treasury Secretary is directed by the statute to prescribe regulations that, among other things, "ensure that individuals required under this law to have an account at a financial institution to receive payments will have access to such an account at a reasonable cost and with the same consumer protections with respect to the account as other account holders at the same financial institution."

This new law takes effect in less than two years. It presents formidable challenges, not only for the Treasury Department, but also for the entire financial services industry. The challenges for Treasury are clear. First, we have to decide how and to what extent we are going to exercise our waiver authority. What does hardship mean? How do we determine what classes of recipients or payments should be excluded from the act without undermining its very purpose? Are we going to get embroiled in litigation over the exercise of that waiver authority or our refusal to grant waivers? We are now looking at all those difficult issues.

We also have the problem of definitions. How do we define "financial institution?" The statute does not say "insured depository institution" or "depository financial institution" or "bank." It says "financial institution." Does that mean that only depository institutions can be selected as payment recipients? To what extent do we have discretion under these definitions to narrow or broaden the concept of financial institutions? Does it have to be an insured institution; i.e., do we have to make sure that FDIC protection is available? Does it have to be regulated at all, or can uninsured, unregulated financial institutions be eligible to be designated as recipients of federal payments?

What is meant by the term, "authorized agent"? Who can qualify as an authorized agent? How is an authorized agent appointed? An authorized agent is presumably something other than a financial institution, since it is articulated separately in the statute. What evidence, if any, do we need of the agency relationship between the individual, and is the authorized agent the individual's agent or is it our agent? What standards of responsibility, if any, do we promulgate for authorized agents?

In many ways these are the typical kinds of problems faced by any agency trying to carry out a broadly stated congressional mandate. But we have one additional challenge which I think is our greatest challenge: defining our responsibility to ensure access to an account. What does that mean? Does that mean that we need to provide an account? Does that mean that we need to require institutions to offer or make available an account for these purposes? Or do we merely have to ensure that reasonable alternatives are available in the marketplace at reasonable cost? But then, how do we determine reasonable cost? What standards of reference do we use to determine whether a product that is being offered, say, by a commercial bank is being offered at a reasonable cost?

We do not have a lot of time to solve these problems — less than two years before the trigger date in the statute arrives. A good part of that time will require a very significant public education campaign to alert recipients of federal payments that they will not receive checks anymore, but instead will receive credits at a financial institution or authorized agent that they designate.

This statute also presents an enormous challenge for the financial services industry. To put it in its broadest terms, how do we provide recipients of electronic payments a share in the enormous cost savings that are going to result from EFT '99? When those rolls of paper disappear at the processing centers and the people who stack those paper checks are employed in other occupations, how do we ensure that the cost savings will enure to the benefit of the recipients? Above all, how do we ensure that recipients will have access to an account?

The paper by Professor Caskey in your background materials is well worth reading. He reports the results of a survey he conducted that indicates that 22 percent of the households surveyed [in several low- and moderate-income areas] did not have bank accounts. We have had estimates that have ranged between 10 percent and 20 percent of households. We also have estimated that more than 10 million regular recipients of federal payments do not have bank accounts.

So we start with a problem. We must deal with a substantial universe, that portion of the unbanked who are recipients of federal payments. A study done several years ago indicated that probably one-third of the households that currently do not have bank accounts are minority-group families, generally with incomes of less than $25,000, so we are dealing with a segment of the population that has distinct, identifiable characteristics. These 10 million or more people now get paper checks every month. They have to incur the cost of cashing those checks. As Professor Caskey points out, 41 percent of the people whom he surveyed who do not have bank accounts pay check cashing fees each month for turning their checks into cash.

People who receive paper checks also run the risk of loss or theft. They are discouraged from saving, because by not dealing with a bank, they do not have an easy way to preserve their funds. There is a tremendous incentive to spend, particularly if they have turned their checks into cash that they carry around. They also do not have an easy means of making third-party payments, such as rent, utility, and other recurring payments each month.

In the past, the problem with bringing formal banking products to this population has been the cost of providing a paper-based account. In recent years, most of the effort to address the need for lifeline banking services has been based on the concept of a paper-based account. That experience, however successful or unsuccessful it may have been in the past, is irrelevant when we are looking at the environment of the future.

The electronic environment offers an opportunity for providing an account at a much lower cost than the traditional paper-based checking account. The electronic account also carries substantial collateral benefits, such as the elimination of the risk of overdrafts, the potential encouragement of savings, the use of other banking products, and the creation of float, all of which will help offset some of the costs of providing the basic service in the first place.

But why should institutions be interested in

> The electronic environment offers ... an account at a much lower cost than the traditional paper-based checking account.

seeking out some of this 10 million or more population? After all, when you divide it up geographically, the average bank will not be able to identify much of a target market, unless it is a larger multistate organization. I submit that profit and business expansion opportunities are a fundamental reason for seeking this market, using the cost savings available in the electronic environment to make money, and still provide a service to the unbanked population that receives federal payments.

Financial institutions should be interested in this market to protect their franchise. If they allow this population to be lured permanently to nonbank intermediaries, they may lose the opportunity to create long-term relationships. Check cashers, data processing companies, and other innovators will find ways to serve this population. They will be competing and trying to find ways to attract this population away from banks and into other forms of payment services.

Finally, it is in the banking industry's enlightened self-interest to meet EFT '99 requirements with a private solution to avoid imposition of government mandates. One does not have to look far back in history to come up with quasi-public utility models that could be brought to bear on the banking system if it ignores the need to provide accounts for the millions of people who are going to need them.

It also seems inevitable that states and private employers will also make their regularly-recurring payments electronically as soon as the superstructure exists to allow them to do so. In existing electronic benefit transfer (EBT) programs in various parts of the country, the states in many cases are already partners with the federal government.

What kinds of services should banks or other financial institutions offer to this population? In the first instance, it has to be up to the marketplace. Institutions need to determine, based on their knowledge of what their customers and potential customers want, what to offer, what is cost-justified, and what fee structure will work without it being a money-losing subsidy to recipients of federal payments.

While the government has an obligation to

ensure access to an account at a reasonable cost, we are reluctant at this stage to define account specifications or to put out any kinds of standards as to what constitutes a reasonable price. If we do that, it will dampen innovation and competition. We would much prefer to see the marketplace come up with a range of solutions to the problem.

The role of the non-depositories is important. Customers may prefer dealing with intermediaries that are not financial institutions. But when we start considering the role of non-regulated, non-insured firms, to what extent should we be concerned about safety and soundness and accountability, and what kinds of standards should we promote in that regard? Moreover, there is nothing to prevent nonfinancial intermediaries from partnering with traditional financial institutions. One could imagine, for example, major data processing firms developing a standardized product that could be offered to smaller depository institutions around the country. That presents a large range of technological problems, but also a great opportunity to act as a kind of a franchiser to attract participants in this market.

The government does not want to be in the business of specifying the attributes of these accounts, as we did in the case of EBT, where the federal government was procuring services in a contract setting. There we specified virtually every aspect of the relationship down to the looks of the card, the pricing of the account, the number of transactions that could be carried out within certain parameters, and every aspect of the entire payment interchange process. We do not want to have to do that for this program, but we may have no other alternative as we watch what is happening in the private sector. We do not have a great deal of time to build up that experience because to launch something like an EBT project requires an enormous amount of lead time.

However, absent some sort of EBT contract model, it will not be appropriate for us to specify the account attributes. Certain attributes, however, do suggest themselves. It seems to me that a debit card-based product would be a fundamental aspect of any account that serves recipients of federal payments. Also important will be a minimum number of withdrawals for a modest charge, or no charge. There may well be an inverse relationship between the number of withdrawals permitted and the profitability

of the account. For example, if only one free withdrawal were allowed, people would be encouraged to pull out all their money at the beginning of the month, which would re-create some of the problems we are trying to avoid with electronic payments, as well as deprive the institution of float opportunities. At the other extreme, permitting unlimited withdrawals means that institutions will incur other kinds of costs. So striking the right balance will be important.

It also seems to me that some third-party payment options will have to be included in these accounts to realize the full benefits of electronic funds transfer. We would hope that the private sector will address that issue.

Furthermore, some of the early indications from the EBT programs are that if recipients do not have to turn their payments at the beginning of each month into cash which they carry around, they will keep something in their accounts and have some savings at the end of the month. This suggests that there are opportunities for financial institutions to offer vehicles to encourage savings.

At Treasury we spend a great deal of time on this. Research is an important part: we have to learn more about the characteristics of the unbanked population who are recipients of federal payments. Public education is another aspect. Our initial estimate vastly understated the amount of investment in public education needed merely to make people aware of what is coming, let alone how they should seek out a service to meet their needs by January 1, 1999. A group is also working on the regulation and will issue a notice of proposed rulemaking that addresses a number of the concerns that I have identified in these remarks. In that process, we will be looking for comments from all of you and other knowledgeable people.

It will be important for us to proceed with a realistic idea of what we are getting into. But it will also be necessary for us to proceed rapidly, because if we determine that a heavier hand of government is needed to meet the statutory requirement of access to an account at a reasonable cost, we will have to move quickly. But our fondest hope is that a thousand flowers will bloom, and that when it comes time to deal with those folks who have not told us where to send their payments, we will be able to direct them to the many offerings that private institutions will be providing to this population.

Reflections on Issues Related to Mandatory EFT '99

EDWARD FURASH, Furash Associates: Whenever the government chooses to make a massive investment in a given technology structure, it creates the capacity for others to ride on it. The banking community must realize that if the government is going to go to electronic benefits transfer and erect the structure to do so, the technology and financial base will be created on which the banking system will build and change. This has happened repeatedly in other forums when other technologies are introduced. So the government, by its spending, could well drive the use of technology in financial services.

MARTIN LIEBERMAN, Community Currency Exchange Association of Illinois: A flurry of activity has begun outside the banking world to involve people who are either ineligible for the banking system, or have chosen not to participate in it. This activity is intended to meet the mandated electronic benefit delivery by 1999. It has also been designed to accommodate various states' attempts to eliminate paper-based systems for the distribution of welfare benefits.

The electronic benefits transfer (EBT) discussed here today has been portrayed as the cheapest, fastest, and safest method; it defies description of how wonderful EBT should be, at least, theoretically. However, the facts about EBT are not yet out on the table. Some of the programs have been implemented in a "vanilla" marketplace, that is, in situations where success is almost guaranteed. Areas where EBT has not yet been tried include rust belt communities, inner cities on the East Coast, areas that have no ATMs or banking facilities, and those that have minimal numbers of supermarkets with point-of-sale registers and other necessary equipment.

The Benefit Delivery Reform Act specified two important points. The first was that access to benefits should not be less than what was available in prior delivery systems. Secondly, the delivery system should maximize the use of small businesses currently involved in the delivery of benefits. Establishments now involved in the delivery should be given every opportunity to participate at a comparable compensatory rate. That is very important: equal access and allowing a fair rate of comparable return to those who now distribute.

JOHN P. CASKEY, Swarthmore College: There are many good arguments for permitting check cashing outlets as delivery points for the receipt of benefit payments. However, many check cashing outlets make loans on the basis of anticipated payments, or "payday loans." This is an old business; the salary purchase business has been around as far back as 1900 to advance people money on the basis of future income.

A payday loan works by the customer writing a personal check for, say, $100 and post-dating it for a week or two hence. The check cashing outlet will give the customer $80 immediately. The interest rate on these payday loans is quite high on an annualized percentage basis — 150 percent is quite common. I am not commenting on whether that is good or bad, since there are good reasons for why interest rates are so high. But if one is a proponent of permitting check cashing outlets as a delivery point for the receipt of benefit payments, one should be aware that many of the check cashing outlets are also in the small loan business.

Expanding Access through Technology

What new products, retail delivery mechanisms, staff training and incentives, organizational structures, and other innovative approaches are helping to serve nonbanked households?

New Technologies to Reach the Nonbanked
Participants discussed new technologies that expand access to financial services.

PAMELA FLAHERTY, Citicorp

I would like to describe some of the things that Citicorp is doing to lower the cost of delivery of financial services and to broaden access to them. Lowering costs and increasing convenience is not an issue that we are interested in for lower-income customers alone, but for all income segments.

We are doing this in a variety of ways. One way that has been alluded to today is partnering with nonprofits that have knowledge and expertise as well as access to some customers with whom we do not currently work, and about whom we may not now have much knowledge. We do this both in this country and overseas.

We have had a longstanding relationship with the National Association of Community Development Loan Funds. We have given them performance-based grants that enable them to set professional standards for the community development loan fund industry and training grants. We have shared technical expertise with them. We also provide loans to their member organizations around the country. We worked with the association last year to develop a near-equity product that they could use as leverage to borrow funds, which they used to lend to their local community development loan funds.

We have also provided performance-based grants to the National Federation of Community Development Credit Unions, working with them to involve the community deve-

43

opment credit unions in the statewide EBT movement. We have a longstanding relationship with ACCION International, a nonprofit active in microfinance in the U.S. and Latin America. Here, too, we have been moving beyond grants into exploring ways in which we can have a business relationship with that group, in which we and they make money, and we help them to achieve scale.

Most banks offer a basic banking account, but many of them are mandated by state legislation and may not meet the needs of the targeted lower-income customers; indeed, many of those who use basic banking accounts are not low-income customers. The industry should design something that satisfies the needs of low-income customers but that also fits the cost structure of banks.

Citicorp has a large EBT business around the country and we look at it as a business opportunity in and of itself. Citibank is involved in the Texas project that was referred to earlier, and we also participate heavily in bidding for the state-level contracts. That is giving us a great deal of experience in moving benefit recipient customers to card-based delivery.

We also partner with other organizations. The delivery mechanisms are not provided solely by Citibank, since in many areas of the country, Citibank does not have retail outlets. We deliver EBT, not only through ATMs, but also through grocery stores, point-of-sale (POS), pharmacies, and check cashers. We also have a pilot program, called "PayTM," that allows certain corporate customers to deliver payroll to employees and that has embedded in it a savings account. It is provided through the employer and is targeted to employees who do not have bank accounts. We believe in electronic delivery through Citibank retail branches, and we have established it for all of our customers.

We believe strongly in consumer education. In our New York branches, we have a full-time team of consumer educators who communicate with current customers and non-Citibank audiences. For example, we are a permanent part of the curriculum at a community college. We teach young adults about to enter the workforce basic banking, how to access credit, and how to use electronic delivery.

We have found exactly what our market research showed, which is that all customer groups will be receptive to the conveniences of electronic delivery, if you take the time and the effort to train people about how to use it.

We have also expended a great effort on addressing the concerns of customer groups about electronic banking. For example, with regard to ATMs, customers, particularly low-income persons, are greatly concerned about security. In the last two years, we have tried to improve lighting and access and installed cameras inside the ATM, so that we can have two-way communications with people in the ATM lobby. We can see and listen to what is going on, and customers can talk to us about their concerns. A byproduct of this effort has been, not only a decrease in robberies, but also a tremendous decrease in scams, which are an issue particularly for the elderly.

We improved our pricing to make our electronic delivery more attractive. In referring to electronic delivery, I mean nonbranch delivery, everything from the telephone to the ATM to the personal computer. Customer usage of electronic and telephone service has increased by 10 to 15 percent overall, and even more in lower-income neighborhoods, where we had less penetration. We have learned the power of educating our current and potential customers, because by taking the time and the effort to train them we have been able to achieve much greater usage.

THOMAS SWIDARSKI, Diebold, Inc.: I would like to support my remarks on payments and delivery systems with some numbers. About 62 billion checks are written annually in the United States, a number that has doubled in the last 10 years. So although movement is occurring in electronic delivery, the infrastructure for checks and other existing payment systems is still strong and in place. The existing delivery system has about 82,000 branches, an increase of 25 percent over the same 10 years. The U.S. has about 140,000 ATMs, which process 890 million transactions a month. Projections indicate that there may be as many as 200,000 ATMs by the year 2000.

The financial industry has the difficult task of supporting the existing infrastructure along with the movement to electronics. Banks still have the traditional physical locations represented by branches, while at the same time they are investing in the alternative electronic delivery system. The cost will have to be borne for both systems, because one does not replace the other. It is more an addition of transactions.

Diebold has worked with some institutions to develop unique ways to use technology to serve the unbanked. For example, Standard Bank of South Africa has created an electronic bank, called E-Bank, in an attempt to align the delivery and the costs associated with delivery services to a specific customer segment. For customers who choose to bank through the E-Bank, Standard Bank will be able to offer a lower minimum balance and a package of services specifically designed for them. The key component is use of an alternative delivery channel. This service has aligned itself nicely with a segment of the population that basically has been underserved and underprivileged over the years.

In addition to improving access to banking, Standard Bank has dealt with illiteracy problems by having a touchstone screen ATM developed that has biometrics built into the software platform. People using the machine can swipe their card and use their fingerprint for identification without needing to enter a personal identification number (PIN). In addition, we developed with the bank a method of leading the customer through a transaction using both voice and graphics. The last I saw, the bank had signed up about 500,000 people in the last year for this account, focusing basically on the unbanked market.

Duke Power provides another example of an innovative use of technology to provide banking services. This utility company, which serves North Carolina, including some very rural areas, encountered many of the same infrastructure issues that banks face in terms of the high cost of delivering service to the unbanked market. It was estimated that about 40 percent of their customers were unbanked. Many customers paid their utility bills in cash, while many others paid by presenting their income check at the payment window and receiving cash back. Duke Power wanted to extend routine transactions beyond normal business hours, so Diebold developed an ATM-like terminal that enables customers to pay their utility bills 24 hours a day, seven days a week, and that also accepts cash for payment.

For four or five months, Diebold has conducted a "remote teller system" pilot with Crestar Bank. This fairly low-tech approach is similar to a drive-up teller window, except that here the customer banks inside the branch. The bank replaced the teller counter with free-standing kiosks in which the customer interacts via video conferencing technology with a teller, who is remotely located in a secure location. A vacuum tube sends the documents back and forth. Already, other banks have started a similar pilot or are thinking of doing so.

Most customer reaction has been positive. Customers are generally served faster. They have the option of reading other messages until they are ready to conduct their transactions. Meanwhile, the teller can serve multiple lanes, much as they do in a drive-up environment, and the bank's costs are lower.

A similar innovation is the use of video conferencing capabilities through ATMs, which are also used as sales kiosks, to carry out noncash functions. The customer can press an icon that brings an expert, such as a mortgage lending expert, to the screen for a dialogue. Here, the customers can interact with an expert, whereas at a branch they probably would deal with generalists. This approach provides an expert to facilitate the more complicated, nonroutine transactions.

Even now, we are seeing considerable experimentation, and some successes, with technology expanding access. I think there will be more movement in that direction in the future.

MARTIN LIEBERMAN, Community Currency Exchange Association of Illinois: As I have mentioned earlier, there are definite advantages to a partnership between check cashers and banks. Check cashers have lower operating costs; better hours, locations, and staff; and a better understanding of the marketplace. Banks, however, can provide check cashers with access to the banking system. This points to the value of a partnership between banks and check cashers.

I would like to tell you about the new products or service delivery methods that are available today or in the developmental stages. In Illinois, my check cashing association and our banking partners, Corus Bankshares and LaSalle National Bank, have created a delivery method to provide federal benefits to recipients, who sign up for the Direct Delivery program, either with the bank or at the check casher's store. The procedures to set up a direct deposit account are identical at either the check casher or the bank.

When the bank receives the electronic benefits on the specified delivery date, it deducts a small fee for account maintenance and sweeps the remainder into a trust account. The benefits are downloaded electronically, and a check is prepared and delivered to the recipient together with the disclosure statement required by Regulation E. Recipients wishing to cash the benefit check pay the current check casher's rate, or otherwise take the check to wherever it will be cashed. The check casher provides a service to the community in that it imposes no charge on checks that are not cashed.

Any check casher in the country could sign up and run this Direct Delivery program by using a modem and simple software. Our intent was to develop a low-cost, quick, efficient program that is applicable anywhere. Customers would continue their present relationship with the neighborhood merchant and still be in full compliance with the federally-mandated EFT by 1999. Customers are not being forced into the banking system.

Banc One has a program on the market today that is similar in concept to the Illinois program. Here, the customer establishes a relationship with Banc One and technology is used to distribute the check locally. The technology is based upon a system of "rapid anticipation" tax refund loans. A system such as this could grow because this platform could support private or governmental payroll checks, as well as state welfare benefits.

Western Union's parent, First Data, is designing a system that would create a national network for the delivery of benefits. This approach would allow recipients to sign onto the network and pick up their benefits at any location that provides Western Union services.

Other similar programs are in their infancy. A partnership between Chase Manhattan Bank and the New York Check Cashers Association, which has 400 members, has evolved into the checks-to-cash club, a point-of-banking system. This system is now in test mode and is due to roll out this summer. While the Illinois system is check-based, the New York program is based on a plastic card. The checks-to-cash club offers a complete menu to the customer to access payroll or welfare benefits, pay bills, transfer between accounts, and obtain balance information. They can do anything that Chase can do, and, in reality, have become an arm of Chase. In effect, there will be 400 new branches of Chase distributed throughout New York City and, to a certain extent, the state.

Another company, Travelers Express, is developing a method for creating an employee payroll. An employee can go into any Travelers Express location and present a card and PIN number. The system produces a paycheck for the employee, who can either cash it there or somewhere else. This system also could be designed to handle the federal mandate for EFT. A person could sign up to have their benefits sent to Travelers Express' bank, and Travelers Express could download the benefits.

One must keep in mind that someone must pay for the cost of delivering the electronic benefits to the community. Change costs money. If the government, in mandating these changes, does not pay for the necessary infrastructure to deliver these benefits, the business community must be allowed to recoup its investment. For years, the people in the communities have chosen to pay a small fee for services rather than travel a long distance for free services. This small fee would support the infrastructure needed to provide the electronic benefit services.

Today, many banks seem to be thinking of trying to fill the void on their own, but the banking world must become comfortable with the check casher as a part of the distribution network. A check casher is similar to a 7-Eleven-style grocery store. Customers know they will pay a premium for their groceries, but the 7-Eleven stores are open late, have small lines, and have become a part of today's urban landscape.

Banks today do not seem to want to build brick-and-mortar branches. Our check cashing facilities are there, so partnership between the two seems to be a logical extension. My industry has always been partners with banks, which have provided us with our services. Banks cash our checks for us, clear items, and provide us with our currency and coin and with technology. It is a logical progression that this relationship continue and expand.

DAVID JOHNSON, Corus Bankshares: I am with Corus Bank and working with Martin Lieberman's group. Corus Bank is a niche bank, with only 12 locations. We are a low-cost provider — our efficiency ratio is a little less than 40 percent. Our bank does more business with check cashers than any other bank in Illinois.

We consider each market segment that we do not yet reach, as if it were any other goal or target. We ask: Is it worth going after? What is the competition like? In Chicago, the check cashers dominate the unbanked section. We would rather cooperate with the check cashers than move in on their territory and lag behind them. Rather than create another option, we prefer to expand upon an existing option, one that has led to partnering.

Under Secretary Hawke commented on corollary objectives, such as a more secure system than the one presently in place. Our approach is secure only as far as receipt of the check. If recipients decide to cash it or carry the check, it is no more or less secure than the existing system. Second, our approach is not likely to encourage savings. Mr. Hawke mentioned that we lose the opportunity to have deposited funds if a paycheck is cashed all at once. This is an economic decision and we must weigh whether it is worth it to us or not. If we say it is not worth it and we are wrong, we face the market consequences. I do not think that it is our responsibility to encourage people to save. People have a free choice of whether they want to save or not.

We do not have a problem with people using checks or with money orders as a payment mechanism. We believe that it is acceptable for the unbanked to pay a check cashing fee. Even though we are not quite advancing to the 21st century, we are taking a practical, pragmatic step.

HAL NIERNBERGER, HALsystem, Inc.: By the end of the century, the paycheck will be replaced mostly by electronic deposit. We are marketing the HALcard to payroll companies, employers, staffing companies, and employee leasing companies to provide direct deposit. We furnish the card and enroll each employee. When I worked in the check cashing business, I determined that the one need that paycheck cashing could not fulfill was the capability to leave one's money somewhere. We provide that capability with the HALcard.

> We would rather cooperate with the check cashers than move in on their territory and lag behind them.

KATHARINE MCKEE, Self-Help: I have been working in the Community Redevelopment Act (CRA) area for many years. Community activists repeatedly note that an ATM is not the same as a brick-and-mortar branch and ask why their communities should not get full service banking.

We have reached the point where we must embrace those aspects of the technology that can really help communities — particularly with accumulating savings — and continue to raise challenges to those aspects of the technology that might harm them. I feel very differently about the use of ATMs or kiosks as a strategy to increase savings than I do about their substitution for bank staff with whom one might discuss a credit request.

Perhaps we should unlink the two and pursue technology to the extent that it lowers costs and helps capture an increased percentage of the unbanked into the savings structure, while also looking for ways to meet their face-to-face lending needs. For the foreseeable future, the alternative financial services providers, both for-profit and nonprofit, may fill those needs.

DOUGLAS FERRIS, National Commercial Bank Services, Inc.: I work for a firm that has financial branches in supermarkets. When we started in-store bank branches about 10 or 11 years ago, nobody thought that they would work. We relied on training and customer education to help consumers understand the in-store banking concept. As a result, we have been able to lend a lot of money in supermarkets, and today are able to sell a variety of other services.

Some interesting and creative ventures are occurring around the world, not necessarily only with the unbanked. In Peru, for example, in-store branches are going into one of the large retail chains there. In Portugal, banking kiosks are being launched through a joint venture between Commercial de Portuguese and a retail partner. It is a 50/50 partnership in which together they offer a telephone system and direct electronic transfer. In the U.K., the Sainsbury Bank has been chartered recently as a joint venture of the Bank of Scotland and

Sainsbury, and another in-store branch is being formed by Abbey National and Safeway (not the U.S. Safeway). You realize that this is a global development.

In order for banks to reach and serve the unbanked, I believe that the unbanked must have the kind of confidence in banks that they have in check cashers today. I do not know if banks will be able to build this credibility on their own as quickly as they can acquire it through partnerships with retailers offering financial services. I also think that we are discussing basically a fee-based business as opposed to a deposit business. It is hard to make the kinds of fees on a $150, $200, or $500 savings account that would be required to offset the cost of cashing checks or performing ATM transactions. ATM deposits are not free:

> We must embrace those aspects of the technology that can really help communities — particularly with accumulating savings — and raise challenges to those aspects of the technology that might harm them.

someone has to pick them up and service the ATMs.

I expect that we may see more joint ventures in the U.S. between banks, check cashers, and retailers where you take the same concept, but perhaps in different packages.

STEVEN RATHGABER, NYCE Corporation: We are working with Chase in New York and Connecticut to install in check cashers point-of-banking terminals for manned electronic access to EBT accounts. This basically lets the unbanked become pseudo-banked. By having an EBT account available at Citibank, for example, customers will be able to access their funds from the NYCE network of about 17,000 ATMs and 70,000 to 90,000 point-of-sale locations. That is a dramatic, practically overnight transition into the 21st century, because of the mandated EBT account.

ROSS LONGFIELD, Beneficial Management Corporation: I agree with much of what Martin Lieberman said, in terms of the opportunity for partnerships between the banking industry and the alternate financial services, including check cashers. I would like to describe briefly an experiment that Beneficial is conducting.

Beneficial is known primarily for the 1,000 consumer finance offices it has around the country. Ironically, the company entered that business in 1914 in circumstances similar to today's, in that banks did not lend to wage earners. Unsecured loans did not exist in 1914. After legislation passed that permitted unsecured lending in a tightly regulated way, Beneficial entered that business and broke new ground.

Since then, we have added other businesses, including a private label credit card operation with major retailers, such as Kmart and Best Buy Superstores. And, through our partnership with H & R Block, we are a dominant player in the tax refund market and we service about 3.5 million customers a year, about 40 percent to 45 percent of whom are unbanked. So we think we have gotten to know that customer.

While we are not a traditional bank, we are a bank holding company and have three charters. One is a charter for a single-purpose credit card bank and another is a commercial bank. As a result of carrying out a treasury function for our 1,000 branch offices and the seasonal tax refund business, Beneficial National Bank performs a lot of transaction processing.

As a result of our experience and the 1999 EFT mandate, we began discussions with In-Person Payments (IPP) about other services we might provide. We expect to launch this program in the first few locations in March. Customers will have an FDIC-insured bank account and receive monthly statements. They can accept direct deposit or other monies into the account. The difference is that they can open an account at locations other than bank branches. The paper check will be eliminated, thereby avoiding overdrafts and cutting account maintenance expenses. The customer can access money through a debit card at NYCE, MAC, Honor, Plus and other debit networks, at retail point-of-sales, and at any IPP location.

MARVIN MORRIS, In-Person Payments Today: IPP has almost 800 locations in Connecticut, New York, New Jersey, Pennsylvania, Maryland, and Washington, D.C. They are small mom-and-pop retail operations, food markets, check cashers, pharmacies, convenience stores — a wide variety of stores. IPP manages those stores, equips them with PC-compatible machines with modems, and provides instructions on how to take payments.

Today, these stores are taking cash payments from customers. They are paying about 180 different types of billers, ranging from phone, gas and electric, catalogues, department store credit cards, virtually any kind of bill. We aim to put in swipe machines to be able to go through NYCE and MAC to Beneficial Bank to handle the debit card transactions. With that card, the customer will be able to access the benefits deposited into the account, buy goods and services, and pay bills.

ROSS LONGFIELD, Beneficial Management Corporation: This product has a payment mechanism, the essential feature of an ideal product, and also satisfies Regulation E. In the

> Customer acceptance will drive the evolution of this technology.

pilot the payment mechanism will not be tightly integrated; we have not found all the answers — we are in the learning stage. The transaction pricing issues that were discussed earlier are relevant, and we are going to have to fine-tune and learn during this process. We also hope to find out about the materiality — can this be done on a scale large enough to make it profitable? Although this product is not without risk, we think it will be an exciting experiment.

THOMAS SWIDARSKI, Diebold, Inc.: New applications of technology include American Express ATMs that dispense travelers checks and, as the checks are dispensed, read the MICR-encoded line. This means that American Express knows which travelers checks you received, as if you completed the same transaction at a typical branch.

Other new applications of technology include companies that are dispensing money orders. The machines are capable of printing a unique money order. Alternatively, the machine could dispense money orders if the machine's cassette were loaded with money

orders instead of cash. 7-Eleven and others have even approached Diebold to turn the ATM into a vending machine. So in the future, you will be able to dispense any item of value, not only cash.

Customer acceptance will drive the evolution of this technology. The technology can support the service once there is a business case for it. But it is important for firms not to be too far out in front.

Consumer Attitudes Toward Technology
Participants also discussed attitudes toward new technology by people in general, and the nonbanked population in particular.

PAUL HAMMOND, Yankelovich Partners: Information on consumer attitudes toward technology is available from the Yankelovich Monitor survey, which has been conducted since 1971. We interview customers for two hours about their attitudes, values, lifestyles, and behaviors. The data base has responses from about 4,000 Americans.

Our survey results revealed, first, that consumers are ambivalent toward technology. They believe that technology is useful only so far as it fits their needs. Consumers like technology if they find its benefits useful, but they do not like technology for itself. We term this response the "microwave test." The microwave is very simple and yet it has immediate and significant benefits. Consumers want technology that works for them, is easy to understand, and does not complicate their life. They believe that their life is already too complicated.

Second, privacy is an overwhelmingly important issue for consumers, one on which they will not compromise. They are afraid that if they give someone else information about their finances, their privacy will be invaded, and this fear constitutes an absolutely fundamental issue.

Thirdly, consumers are feeling stressed and are trying to streamline their lives. They blame their excessive stress on overload: too many "to do's." They implement control in one of three ways. If something is important, they will keep it. If they can live without it, they will jettison it. And they look for strategic partners to help them manage their lives. Their confidence in financial planners has increased in recent years. Consumers want partners who will help give them control and whose advice and information resonates with them as accurate and useful.

The risk of technology is the risk of invasion of privacy. Providers must assemble safeguards and explain to consumers that their privacy is inviolate if they use technology to carry out their finances. Also, consumers, in seeking control and reassurance, still need a human being with whom to discuss their finances. They cannot do this solely through an ATM or over the phone.

Manned ATMs are an example of technology that provides easy access and still enables consumers to talk about finances with a human being. That is not possible with an automated response on the phone, a computerized system, or an unmanned ATM. Although we want to shift as rapidly as possible into a technologically-advanced era, the consumers are holding the industry back, because they still want contact with human beings. Increasingly, consumers will select banks on the basis of user-friendly technology and the option for personal contact.

THOMAS NORTON, Western Union North America: As a provider that spends a lot of time and effort in this area of technology, I am dubious about cost reduction through technology. Our experiences in the marketplace continue to support the Yankelovich findings about the consumer's ambivalence about technology and the need for a partner.

We have an incredible amount of money invested in a voice response unit (VRU) that allows people to call us up and check on the status of their transactions. Significantly, to find that telephone number, you have to be able to read the Yellow Pages, so these customers are not illiterate. They immediately bang their way past the VRU. They want to hear a voice tell them what they were already told at the retail level. They need that assurance.

In the last few years, we have built an extremely large, in-person utility bill payment business, which accepts both checks and cash. We see people with checking accounts who will walk into a retail location and hand over a check because they want to hear the response to their questions, "I'm paid, right?" "Yes." "So when does this money get there?" "It gets there

tonight at midnight, maybe one o'clock." "They're not going to shut me off, right?" It is that risk aversion/control element that costs us systemwide money every day. I would love to find a machine that would get me past that.

JIM MEADOWS, Citizens National Bank: As I mentioned earlier, we are a one-unit bank and our customer base is primarily ethnic and low-to moderate-income. One of the most difficult things we have had to do, and we still have not

> Increasingly, consumers will select banks on the basis of user-friendly technology and the option for personal contact.

got it right, is to teach people how to use a checking account. We take for granted being able to fill out the check and write out the numbers in English, and being able to balance a bank statement, but our customers have a hard time with this.

We have had some success in moving people into certain types of technology. We have had people latch onto the ATM and telephone access system, once they figure it out. Through pricing, we have induced people to use the telephone, allowing us to successfully off-load some costs. For a small bank, we have an enormous number of transactions by telephone: some 20,000 a month for a $50 million bank.

NANCY BARRY, Women's World Banking: We work with low-income women entrepreneurs in over 50 countries of Africa, Asia, Latin America, Europe, and North America. Commercial banks often fulfill a wholesale function for our affiliates, who are the specialized retailers. We also actively encourage commercial banks to become directly involved in retailing savings and lending services to those in the lowest 30 percent of the population.

The only way to prevent the 14 percent of the unbanked population from becoming the 30 percent is through technology. The large banks say that essentially they do not make any money on the low end of banking: It costs them $150 per year per account and they are certainly not getting that in revenue. So those of us who care about that bottom 30 percent have to work with the banks to figure out ways to extend technology with innovations and outreach.

The overseas microfinance industry is moving toward what the management literature terms "operational excellence," meaning lowest cost, standardized producer. They keep it quick, and they keep it simple. For example, in South Africa, banks and some nonprofit organizations have become highly automated, where one staff member can make thousands of loans. They do not care about the purpose for which the money is borrowed. The customer borrows $100; if it is repaid, the customer can borrow $200; if that is repaid, the customer can borrow $400. But, on the other hand, there is the view that the customer relationship is important. It is important to the customer and for the microfinance lender, which earns its money with repeat clients.

The approach to banking with the poor in the United States will be different than it is overseas. I am sure that we underestimate this population's capacity and propensity to save, and it will be important to redress that issue. We will also need a lower-cost solution to lending if the banks are going to become involved. Otherwise, I think that the growth segment of this business will be the pawn brokers, check cashers, and other institutions that have the high-touch approach. It is clear that the unbanked are willing to pay high fees for the kinds of services that they do not receive from the commercial banks.

JOE BELEW, Consumer Bankers Association: I have one observation on adapting and technological literacy. There are all kinds of technology, and it strikes me that many of the populations that we are talking about may be the earliest adapters of technology, not the latest. You do not have to know the computer language, DOS, to buy a farecard on Washington D.C.'s Metro system. Some immigrant populations are the ones that most often use phone cards and stored value cards.

We run a danger when we think of technology as a big, intimidating, complex creature, rather than as variants that are user-friendly, simple, and expeditious. I think we tend to expect an aspect of intimidation that sometimes might not be there.

KATHARINE MCKEE, Self-Help: Technology must always be looked at in its context. You could have a very low-touch technology, but it could be located where a person can answer the customer's questions, or it could enable the customer to make a phone call. For example, video-conferencing may provide the customer with a surrogate rather than having a person present, but it provides access to expertise that otherwise would not be available at the branch.

Similarly, in a high-touch environment, we should think of whether there are low-touch elements that could add services, increase cost-effectiveness, or improve things for the consumer. It is not merely a case of either/or, or of high-tech or high-touch.

STEPHEN BROBECK, Consumer Federation of America: Just a brief comment on the potential of technology for serving the unbanked. My recollection from the literature on illiteracy is that it ranges in our society from 10 percent to 20 percent, and it is highly correlated with the unbanked. Most of the people who are functionally illiterate have low and moderate incomes, and a disproportionate number of them are minorities. Except for the age distribution, this is also the population that is disproportionately represented among the unbanked.

This raises the question: How does new technology serve that population? If it is print screen-based as opposed to voice-based, it will not meet their needs effectively, unless some kind of assistance is rendered, which introduces a lot of cost.

PAMELA FLAHERTY, Citicorp: There is a tendency to think of non-branch delivery as being fancy electronics, but the phone is also a relevant part of all this. Even in an EBT environment, which is not a full relationship, customers always have the opportunity to talk. All of our EBT customers have access to a toll-free 800 customer service telephone number, and all training (including ways of reaching people to train them) is done through a combination of media.

STEPHEN BROBECK, Consumer Federation of America: Although this solves much of the problem, I recollect from a different set of statistics that 7 percent of all households do not have phones. In certain areas, up to 20 percent, 25 percent, or 30 percent of low-income households do not have phones. I see this as a generational problem, a transitional problem, because it is the older people who are most resistant to new technology and who are most comfortable with having that face-to-face contact at a branch.

MARTIN LIEBERMAN, Community Currency Exchange Association of Illinois: I do not believe that there is a direct correlation between the nonbanked and the illiterate. While I do not have statistics and studies, I do have 40 years of experience dealing daily with people who do not use banks. I can assure you that they are neither illiterate nor dysfunctional. They have merely chosen, for a myriad of reasons, not to use a bank.

EDWARD FURASH, Furash Associates: I suggest that our conversation may need a framework. We should keep three key points in mind when we discuss the migration of financial services to broaden access through technology.

First, consumer financial services are, in their essence, a form of retailing. Although it may wax and wane, no retailing function ever disappears. So, for example, when all the mom-and-pop grocery stores disappeared, because they were uneconomical, they were merely replaced with more-economical 7-Elevens, which carried out the functions of long hours and convenience. Similarly, the financial functions that people need to live their lives are not going to disappear. Who performs them will change. We must recognize that we are dealing with essentially a form of retailing and marketing.

Second, in the financial services sector, consumer behavior is driven fundamentally by the management of unanticipated consequences. Consumers tend to manage risk according to what they perceive to be the risk of the activity they are going to undertake. They manage this risk on five or six dimensions. The functional risk of the activity is whether the product or service performs as expected. Financial risk relates to whether the service is worth its cost, or whether it will damage me financially. Physical risk is whether it will harm me. Psychological risk is whether it fits my self-image or gives me dignity. And another is social risk; that is, is it socially acceptable to do it this way?

> The history of technology adoption... demonstrates that toys become tools; the novelty becomes the necessity.

Using these consumer risk management dimensions demonstrates that all activities have different levels of perceived risk. Buying a tube of toothpaste is a very low perceived risk on the part of the consumers. You spend two dollars and you are counting on the FDA to make sure that the toothpaste will not remove the enamel from your teeth. You do not have to confess to your brother-in-law that you used a bad brand of toothpaste; you just throw it away. This is an example of a decision that is perceived to be low risk.

Financial behavior is probably one of the highest perceived risk activities that consumers undertake. For example, you do not want to tell your brother-in-law that you overpaid for a loan. You do not want to tell somebody that you went to a pawn shop. There are many dimensions on which financial services are perceived to be high risk.

Consumers develop personal strategies for managing perceived risk. One of the reasons for the need for a "high-touch" approach in the adoption of technology is not because people love high-touch per se, but because consumers see it as a method for managing risk — it provides reassurance to consumers. How many of you, when you call a business on the telephone, are gratified that someone will give you their name so that you can get back to them? These are all consumer risk management devices. So the management of perceived risk is the second factor in inducing people to adopt financial technology.

Thirdly, we should also be aware of the history of technology adoption, which demonstrates that toys become tools; the novelty becomes the necessity. The telephone was a toy; it is now a tool. The microwave was a toy; it is now ubiquitous. So toys become tools. The secret in technology adoption is to create for the customer the sense that he or she is using a toy. The toy makes it simple and turns the technology into a tool.

In financial services, we have yet to create the right toys. Banking by personal computer is still too complex. We are asking people to do too much with these new services. But as soon as these services become toys, let me assure you, they will become tools. As they become tools, they will become familiar. And when they are familiar, a consumer will understand how to manage risk and will require less and less personal interaction. We went through this same cycle with ATMs. People would not use them unless someone taught them how.

New York Air experienced a similar situation when it put in automatic ticketing machines that were a wonder of science. You put your card in, punched in a couple of items, and within about 60 seconds out came a ticket. The problem was that these machines were absolutely silent, and so no one thought that they were working. So New York Air hired psychologists to stand beside the machines to tell people that they worked. After that, the company merely installed in each machine an artificial noise that whirred, clicked, and made you think that the machines were operating.

We should always remember that we are dealing with basic human behavior and emotions. If we want to do things for people or have them do what we want, the systems we display must be fun. When they are fun, access broadens quickly. As we look into this new century, we must recognize that this technology is going to cut costs, but it is also going to enable the unbanked to become more complete members of our society. To do so, we have to make it fun for them and cost-effective to bankers.

The Role of Consumer Education
Several participants discussed the importance of consumer education to consumer acceptance of technology.

EUGENE LUDWIG, Office of the Comptroller of the Currency: I am curious about consumer education. I visited a halfway house for drug rehabilitation in New York where Citicorp provided training in financial services. The classes teach people who are re-entering society how to manage their financial needs. The clients asked some pretty sophisticated questions, and many seemed to benefit from the training. What kind of hands-on training do you see as useful, valuable, or necessary for low- and moderate-income people generally, and specifically as we move into a more technological environment?

RICHARD JUAREZ, MAAC Project: We had a grant for two years from Bank of America to run these types of classes and they worked very well, especially for senior populations and for monolingual people. Perhaps Bank of America should have run their own classes and developed that relationship with their customers, rather than giving us that grant, but it was a positive experience for us.

KATHARINE MCKEE, Self-Help: Perhaps training is too formal a word to use, but we CDFIs manage risk through the nonfinancial services we offer. These services help gain customer acceptance for new ways of doing things, and they build relationships. I would say that those services are key: they are the value that we add.

DONALD NEUSTADT, Ace Check Cash Express, Inc.: In my check cashing business we put our technology "behind the window." We focus our training on our employees, making it their responsibility to share the training with consumers, so that they can get the satisfaction out of the product or services that they are purchasing.

When we first installed some of our POS equipment, we also tried to make it fun. Employees could call in and get their horoscope in the morning. We were trying to make it fun so that people would stop being intimidated and work with the technology. We found it effective to focus our training dollars on our employees, rather than going out and training consumers, as Citicorp does.

PAMELA FLAHERTY, Citicorp: We believe that training has been important, but that two issues should be recognized. First, our training is not exclusively oriented toward lower-income people. We have discovered that people in some high-traffic, upper-income areas also need training, particularly in the new kinds of banking.

Second, not everyone wants or desires this hands-on kind of training. In some of the statewide EBT programs, some people will opt to save time by getting their personal identification code and card through the mail, rather than obtaining them in person. Still, there is a tremendous need for consumer education on electronics, credit, and the basics of conducting financial affairs.

Closing Remarks

EUGENE LUDWIG, Comptroller of the Currency

Richard Hartnack and I will summarize a few of the basic themes from today's conference. It will be a collaborative effort as it was in developing this conference. In the first session of the forum, Robert Townsend provided an interesting combination of the economics and statistical analysis of a particular community in Chicago, the results of some fascinating research. His research revealed that although we have learned some things from studying this community, we are only beginning to understand this population.

From the subsequent discussion, we learned that households value personal contact and privacy, and that they have some ambiguity about their openness to new technology. In trying to determine the private sector's response, one theme that emerged again and again throughout the day was the need for a balancing act between the personal touch and new technologies. It will probably take continuing efforts, debate, and study to find that right balance.

A number of participants raised the issue of a savings gap, or a gap in the savings vehicles available to low- and moderate-income people, and the costs that arise from that gap in terms of individual opportunity and economic development.

RICHARD HARTNACK, Union Bank of California

In summing up the barriers to service that were addressed in the second session of the day, two overriding themes emerge. One is rapid change in the banking and financial services industry, as institutions have had to manage their costs and their delivery channels better. The tremendous pressure on costs is changing the way banking services are delivered. Indeed, many of the approaches that we accepted only a few short years ago as routine and accepted, are no longer routine.

The second theme, which John Hawke described at lunch

and which dominates the conversation, are the government's mandatory electronic payments initiatives. In the not-too-distant future, tens of millions of people who are currently unbanked must have somewhere to put their money.

Against that backdrop, we discussed the barriers to getting people into the banking system. One of the first things that we discussed was

> There is a need for
> a balancing act
> between the personal touch
> and new technologies.

whether, in fact, there even is a problem. That question was not answered today; clearly, there are thoughtful people around this table who would say that this population is not really underserved, it is merely served differently.

Even the term "barriers" connotes that people are stuck in some dysfunctional segment of the economy; that may not be true at all. Points were made about savings and the fact that savings accounts can be opened at banks, but not at some of the alternative institutions. This makes it worthwhile to keep looking at the issue of savings and whether there are barriers.

The first barrier is the people themselves, those who have chosen not to be bank customers. This barrier will require substantial change, but it is not yet clear who is going to pay for educating, training, or influencing people to want to change — if, indeed, changing them is good for social policy.

The second barrier clearly is the perception by some banks that this population may present a serious profit challenge. Seamus McMahon threw some light on that, saying that it is probably more a matter of how we price and the way the client behaves than the absolute economics of the circumstance.

Another barrier identified is the corporate culture of banks. Banks already have the 88 percent of the population who are their customers to worry about, and most of them probably believe that they have their hands full merely staying ahead of the competition. There are probably certain barriers in trying to bring along the 12 percent who are still outside the banking system.

Regulatory barriers have existed historically

and may continue to challenge us in developing partnerships and alliances with nonbank institutions. David Johnson and Martin Lieberman described how a bank and a check casher can work together. Other opportunities include savings alliances that will require flexibility by regulators. Certainly, the OCC has indicated an interest in understanding those barriers and working with us to see how they might be effectively addressed.

Finally, Edward Furash described very capably that technology has to be taken seriously. It is one part of the industry that is moving quickly, so it is important to understand how we bring customers along, and what technologies are going to be useful to them, and what will be easily accepted. We will try to achieve good social policy and good economic policy, and yet respect the free market in which people choose the way they want to do business.

EUGENE LUDWIG, Comptroller of the Currency: In the forum's third session, there seemed to be a general view around the room that we are going to see a very changed technological environment for banking as we move into the next century.

Although some may differ as to the degree to which that is a good thing, there seems to be a very little disagreement that change is coming. Participants seemed to believe generally that it is incumbent upon us to make technology our friend, even though there may be different views as to how to do that. One common view was that it need not be off-putting but should be, in fact, simple. Edward Furash's notion that

> ...the costs that arise
> from a savings gap
> in terms of individual opportunity
> and economic development.

if technology can be looked on as a toy, it soon becomes a tool, was insightful.

Despite considerable discussion about consumer education, I do not think we ever entirely agreed about how much education will be needed, either with respect to the new technology or with respect to the unserved or underserved population. Some believe that we need a considerable amount of education, while others seem to believe that the unbanked are making rational judgments, given the economics of their situation.

Surprisingly, we heard common views on partnerships. In this changing world, a patchwork quilt of arrangements and partnerships will probably evolve that will serve different populations somewhat differently in various parts of the country.

In terms of our next steps, the OCC will give some serious thought to the kind of study we might carry out to follow up on the many themes that have been discussed here. Joe Belew and I also plan to convene a group next year to see where these developments have taken us, particularly as the mandatory EFT '99 approaches.

Participant Biographies

Nancy M. Barry

Nancy M. Barry is president of Women's World Banking (WWB), which serves low-income women entrepreneurs. She is responsible for managing effective operations of WWB and for maintaining its fiduciary integrity. She has been a member of WWB's board of trustees since 1981 and was vice chairwoman from 1988 to 1990, before being appointed president. Before joining WWB, Barry spent 15 years with the World Bank, where she pioneered its involvement in small enterprises and designed operations in Asia, Latin America, and Africa. Until September 1990, she led the Industry Development Division, and from 1988 to 1990, she chaired the Donor's Committee on Small and Medium Enterprises. Barry has a B.A. degree in economics from Stanford and a master's of business administration from Harvard University.

Joe Belew

Joe Belew is president of Consumer Bankers Association, a national financial trade association specializing in retail banking issues. As the chief executive officer of the association, Belew directs all activities of the organization, speaks frequently to national audiences on current financial issues, and has appeared on national television shows. He also testifies before Congress on banking issues. He served on the staff of the U.S. Congress for 10 years and on the U.S. Senate staff for three years. He has been a member of the Society of International Business Fellows since 1984 and is a member of the Key Industry Advisory Committee of the American Society of Association Executives. He also serves on the board of directors of the Social Compact. Belew holds a bachelor's degree in public relations and journalism from the University of Georgia in Athens.

Stephen Brobeck

Stephen Brobeck has served as executive director of the Consumer Federation of America (CFA) since 1980. CFA is a federation of 250 groups with more than 50 million members and is the nation's largest consumer advocacy organization. Brobeck has served as visiting professor of consumer economics at Cornell University and as adjunct professor of consumer economics at the University of Maryland. Brobeck graduated from Wheaton College and earned a Ph.D. from the University of Pennsylvania.

Richard S. Carnell

Richard S. Carnell was sworn in as assistant secretary of the Treasury for financial institutions in 1993. In that position, he advises the secretary, the deputy secretary, and the under secretary for domestic finance on all matters relating to financial institutions. He directs policy on proposed legislation and regulation of private financial intermediaries and Treasury activities relating to other federal regulatory agencies. Before joining the Treasury Department he was senior counsel with the Senate Banking Committee from 1989. Carnell graduated from Harvard Law School and earned a B.A. magna cum laude from Yale University.

John P. Caskey

John P. Caskey is an associate professor of economics at Swarthmore College. He received a B.A. from Harvard University and a Ph.D. from Stanford University. His research focuses on financial institutions serving low-income households and on topics in community economic development. He is the author of *Fringe Banking: Check-Cashing Outlets, Pawnshops, and the Poor*. Caskey is a member of the Family Selection Committee of the Chester Community Improvement Project, a not-for-profit low-income housing development agency in Chester, Pennsylvania. He is also a member of the board of directors of the Franklin Mint Federal Credit Union and is a visiting scholar at the Federal Reserve Bank of Philadelphia.

Kevin M. Colosia

Kevin M. Colosia, director of strategic marketing, has been with Motorola for 24 years. He has held various positions of progressive responsibility in technical, marketing, and business development activities for telecommunications products and services. His primary emphasis is on cellular communications systems and services, with additional experience in mobile data, telepoint, wireless local loop, and personal communications networks. Colosia has a B.S. and a graduate degree in electrical engineering from the University of Illinois and a graduate degree in business administration from Northern Illinois University.

Constance R. Dunham

Constance R. Dunham is a senior financial economist at the Office of the Comptroller of the Currency, where she currently heads the agency's "Expanding the Financial Frontiers" project on nonbanked households. Previously, she was senior economist for domestic finance and overseas development issues at the President's Council of Economic Advisers. At the U.S. Agency for International Development, she managed the agency's principal project on microenterprise and small business finance and development. Previously, at the Urban Institute and the Federal Reserve Bank of Boston, Dr. Dunham carried out policy research and wrote numerous articles on U.S. and overseas banking and methods of expanding access to finance. She holds a Ph.D. in economics from Stanford University and B.A. in economics from Yale University.

Douglas W. Ferris, Jr.

Douglas W. Ferris, Jr. serves as president of National Commerce Bank Service (NCBS) Inc., the supermarket banking affiliate of National Commerce Bancorporation (NCBC), a $4.2 billion institution headquartered in Memphis, Tennessee. NCBS provides comprehensive in-store banking consulting services to other financial institutions and supermarkets in the U.S. He has spent nearly 30 years with NCBC and has led the NCBS consulting group since 1987. As president of NCBS, he is a member of the bank's executive committee and is responsible for the strategic direction of the group. Ferris is a graduate of the University of Alabama and of the Stonier School of Banking at Rutgers University.

Pamela P. Flaherty

Pamela P. Flaherty, senior vice president of Citi-corp, is responsible for global community activities in the 98 countries in which the corporation operates. She is the senior CRA officer in the United States and the corporate state officer for Citicorp's businesses in New York. She has held a variety of management positions at Citicorp, including head of the New York consumer business, and head of human resources for Citicorp. A cum laude graduate of Smith College, Flaherty received a master's degree in international relations from the Johns Hopkins School of Advanced International Studies. She is a board member of the American Women's Economic Development Corporation, Organization Resource Counselors, Rockefeller and Company, World Lending, the Consumer Bankers Association, Community Preservation Corporation, and the Local Initiatives Support Corporation. She also serves on the Neighborhood Housing Services New York Advisory Board.

Robert E. Friedman

Robert E. Friedman is founder and chairman of the board of the Corporation for Enterprise Development (CFED), a Washington, D.C.-based not-for-profit economic development research, technical assistance, and demonstration company. For 16 years, Friedman and CFED have worked extensively with public and private policy makers in state and local governments, corporations, private foundations, labor unions, and community groups to design and implement innovative and effective economic development strategies. CFED's work emphasizes job creation through enterprise development. Currently, Friedman is director of CFED West in San Francisco. He was founding chairman of the Association for Enterprise Opportunity and a director of the Levi Strauss Foundation. He is a graduate of Harvard College and Yale Law School.

Philip J. Friedrich

Philip J. Friedrich is a senior consultant with a primary focus on strategic issues, management problem solving and decision making, and project management at Kepner-Tregoe. Previously, he was director of human resources and organizational development for a large government organization. Friedrich's primary work is in the service industry, where he works with commercial banks, and life, health, and property/casualty insurance companies. He did his undergraduate work at Villanova University and graduate work at Pennsylvania State University.

Edward E. Furash
Edward E. Furash founded Furash & Company in 1980. He has advised major financial trade associations, including the American Bankers Association, Robert Morris Associates, the Bank Marketing Association, the Consumer Bankers Association, The Bankers Roundtable, and many state banking associations. Before forming his practice, Furash served nearly 12 years as a senior vice president at the Shawmut Corporation, and subsequently was managing associate and member of the board of directors of Golembe Associates. Furash graduated magna cum laude from Harvard College and received his master's of business administration from The Wharton School, University of Pennsylvania. He was on the faculty of The Wharton School and the Harvard Business School, an assistant editor of the *Harvard Business Review,* and worked as a senior staff associate and business manager with Arthur D. Little Inc.

Donald V. Hammond
Donald V. Hammond was appointed deputy fiscal assistant secretary in 1996 and is responsible for policy oversight for activities in the Financial Management Service and the Bureau of the Public Debt. The office also serves as the Treasury Department's liaison with the Federal Reserve System. The scope of the office's responsibilities includes managing the government's cash flow, accounting for the government's borrowing, and maintaining centralized reporting systems for the government's financial activity. Hammond leads the Treasury working group, which is implementing the requirement to make all federal payments electronically by January 1999. Previously, he was the assistant director of the Treasury Department's government securities relations staff. Hammond has a master's degree in finance and accounting from Northwestern University

and a bachelor's in chemistry and economics from Duke University.

Paul F. Hammond
Paul F. Hammond directs all product development, marketing, and sales activities for Yankelovich Partners' multi-sponsored studies. He has had overall responsibility for syndicated tracking studies of building and design products, retail products, environmental services, commercial office, kitchen and bath, residential remodeling, home mortgage and consumer credit markets, as well as numerous others. Hammond graduated with a B.A. from Brown University and a M.A. from New York University.

Richard C. Hartnack
Richard C. Hartnack is vice chairman, a member of the board of directors, and head of the community banking group at Union Bank of California, which has $27 billion in assets. He joined the bank in June 1991 from the First National Bank of Chicago, where he served as an executive vice president and head of the community banking group. Hartnack began his banking career in 1971. He received an economics degree from UCLA and a master's degree in business administration from Stanford University. Hartnack serves on the boards of the Bank Administration Institute and Independent Colleges of Southern California, is chairman of the Pacific Coast Banking School board of directors, chairman of the California Community Reinvestment Corporation's Board of Directors, and chairman of the Consumer Bankers Association. He also serves on the U.S. region board of directors for MasterCard International and is a member of the California Club and the Economic Club of Chicago. He is also a founding director of California Economic Development Lending Initiative.

John D. Hawke, Jr.
John D. Hawke, Jr., the Under Secretary of the Treasury for Domestic Finance, oversees the development of policy and guides Treasury activities in the domestic finance area. He is the department's chief operating officer and is a member of the President's Management Coun-

cil, which coordinates programs initiated by the National Performance Review that improve the efficiency and customer service of the government. He graduated from Yale University in 1954 with a Bachelor of Arts and in 1960 from Columbia University School of Law, where he was editor of the Columbia Law Review.

David H. Johnson, III

David H. Johnson has been with Corus Bankshares (formerly River Forest Bancorp) for more than five years. He is the executive vice president of the holding company, executive vice president and chief operation officer of Corus Bank (the banking subsidiary), and chairman of Corus Financial. He previously had 12 years with Ernst & Young, most recently as partner in charge of bank consulting in the Midwest region. He has co-authored several books and given numerous speeches on the banking industry. Johnson graduated from the University of Kansas with an undergraduate business degree and a master's of business administration.

Julia F. Johnson

Senior Vice President Julia F. Johnson joined Bank One Columbus 12 years ago. Johnson was named to her current position as Community Reinvestment Act (CRA) officer of Banc One Corporation in 1986 and oversees implementation of all affiliate bank CRA programs. Johnson is also a director of the Banc One Community Development Corporation and Finance One Corporation. She serves as a member of the Community Reinvestment Committee of the Consumer Bankers Association and the Riverfront Commons Corporation and serves as a director of the W.B. Marvin Mfg. Company of Urbana, Ohio. She is also a member of the board of trustees of Kenyon College.

Richard Juarez

Richard Juarez has been involved in inner-city community development in San Diego for more than 25 years. He is director of the Community Development Department of the Metropolitan Area Advisory Committee (MAAC), a multiservice community-based nonprofit orga-

nization. Juarez serves on the board of directors of the Southeastern Economic Development Corporation and the city's Redevelopment Agency. He also serves on the board of the California Community Economic Development Association, the board of the New California Economic Development Lending Initiative Bank, the senior advisory board of the San Diego Neighborhood Development Association, and the board of the Environmental Health Coalition. He was a founding member and first president of the San Diego Nonprofit Federation for Housing and Community Development.

Martin A. Lieberman

Martin A. Lieberman is a director of the Community Currency Exchange Association (CCEA) of Illinois Inc., which represents an estimated 700 check cashers. He has been a director since 1975 and is responsible for creating new products and management techniques for CCEA members. Lieberman has been a director of the National Check Cashers Association, which represents more than 3,000 members in 35 states, since its inception in 1986. He is also president and general manager of Central Clearing Company, a chain of nine currency exchange stores in the Chicago area. The company also operates 14 locations in Michigan, with a special emphasis on welfare benefits. Lieberman has a B.S. in accounting, with special emphasis on management systems, from DePaul University.

Ross N. Longfield

As senior vice president of Beneficial Management Corporation, Ross N. Longfield is president of two subsidiaries: Beneficial Tax Masters Inc. and Beneficial National Bank USA. He also leads Beneficial International Card Services, a management group formed in 1996 to oversee Beneficial's international credit card business. Longfield began his career with Beneficial while attending Fairleigh Dickerson University in 1960. In 1982 he was named president of Beneficial Tax Masters Inc.; in 1990 he became president of Beneficial National Bank USA; and two years later was named to his current position.

Eugene A. Ludwig

Eugene A. Ludwig took the oath of office on April 5, 1993, as the 27th Comptroller of the Currency. By statute, the Comptroller serves a concurrent term as a director of the Federal Deposit Insurance Corporation and is chairman of the Neighborhood Reinvestment Corporation. The Comptroller also serves as a member of the Federal Financial Institutions Examination Council. Ludwig joined the OCC from the law firm of Covington and Burling in Washington, D.C., where he was a partner beginning in 1981. He specialized in intellectual property law, banking, and international trade. He earned a B.A. magna cum laude from Haverford College. He also received a Keasbey scholarship to attend Oxford University, where he studied politics, philosophy, and economics, and earned a B.A. and M.A. He also holds an L.L.B. from Yale University, where he served as editor of the *Yale Law Journal* and chairman of Yale Legislative Services.

James M. McCormick

James M. McCormick is president and a founder of First Manhattan Consulting Group (FMCG), a financial industry consulting firm. He is also president of FMCG Capital Strategies. McCormick has 18 years of experience consulting to financial industries in a variety of subjects and has been called to testify before the Senate Banking Committee. He holds master's and bachelor's degrees from Cornell University.

Katharine W. McKee

Katharine W. McKee has been a senior manager since 1986 with the Self-Help development banking group, one of the most successful community development financial institutions. Self-Help was created in 1980 to provide economic opportunities to low-income, rural, female, and minority North Carolinians. In 1994, McKee was appointed by the Clinton Administration to the position of transition director for the newly created Community Development Financial Institutions Fund, which was established to provide capital, technical assistance, training, and related support to existing and start-up community development financial institutions nationwide. Before joining Self-Help, she spent eight years as a program officer with the Ford Foundation. McKee has just completed a three-year term on the Consumer Advisory Council of the Board of Governors of the Federal Reserve. She is a graduate of Bowdoin College and has a master's degree in public and international affairs from Princeton University.

Seamus McMahon

Managing Vice President of First Manhattan Consulting Group, Seamus McMahon has spent the last 17 years as a consultant to management in the financial services industry. McMahon has worked primarily in consumer, small business, and middle market segments where he focuses on revenue generation and restructuring distribution. He has a bachelor's degree in economics and a masters of arts degree from Trinity College, Dublin.

Jim P. Meadows

Jim P. Meadows is chairman and chief executive officer of Citizens National Bank in Houston, Texas. He has 20 years of experience as a community bank chief executive officer (CEO) in Texas. Meadows earned a degree in economics from Texas Christian University and received a law degree from the University of Georgia Law School.

Lisa Mensah

Lisa Mensah is deputy director of the Economic Development Unit in the Asset Building and Community Program at the Ford Foundation. In this capacity, she is responsible for negotiating grants totaling over $2 million annually to community development financial institutions that help create small enterprises and other employment opportunities in the United States and in developing countries. Prior to joining the Ford Foundation in 1989, Mensah worked in corporate finance for Citibank in New York. She holds a M.A. in international studies from Johns Hopkins University and a B.A. in government from Harvard University.

Marvin A. Morris

Marvin A. Morris is the president and founder of In-Person Payments, which is a three-year-old electronic payment services company. Before founding IPP, Morris was the regional vice president for National Payments Network, which processed in-person payments for several utilities and was eventually sold to Western Union. Morris is a graduate of City College of New York in computer science. He is also an associate member of the New Jersey Check Cashers Association.

Donald H. Neustadt

Donald H. Neustadt has served as president and chief executive officer of Ace Cash Express Inc. (ACE) since November 1994 and previously served as a director beginning in January 1987. ACE, the largest chain of retail financial service stores in the U.S., was founded in 1968. From 1984 to 1985, Neustadt served as president of Associates Financial Express, Inc., where he was one of three people to negotiate the purchase of ACE in 1984. Neustadt received a B.A. in economics from the University of Illinois and an MBA from Loyola University, Chicago.

Hal Niernberger

Hal Niernberger, is the founder, chairman, chief executive officer, and president of HAL-system Inc. Prior to founding HALsystem, Niernberger founded Money Mart Check Cashing Centers in 1968. Money Mart was one of the first check cashing companies to serve the market in a dignified and system-based manner. The company was acquired in 1984 by The Associates. At the time, the company was a multimarket system of 75 retail financial centers. The company is now Ace Cash Express, the nation's largest check cashing company with more than 600 stores.

Thomas P. Norton

Thomas P. Norton is the vice president and business manager of Consumer Products for Western Union North America. He develops card-based products, manages the customer data base, and starts other businesses capitaliz-ing on First Data Corporation (FDC) competencies and Western Union market strengths. Norton has also worked as the eastern region vice president where he managed a field team selling the Western Union portfolio. Previously, he worked for Citicorp and Maxwell House Coffee Company in corporate level sales, marketing, and general management positions.

Roger W. Raina

Roger W. Raina is a co-founder of National Item Processing Inc., which was established in 1992 to give companies a cost-effective method for clearing checks, drafts, or money orders. Raina has more than 30 years experience in banking, including operations management, correspondent banking, cash management, and consulting as well as courier service management. In 1984 he founded, and remains president of, Roger W. Raina & Associates Inc., which provides cash management and operations consulting to financial institutions and financial services companies. Before that, Raina purchased and operated a small commercial printer that specialized in printing for financial institutions. The company was sold in 1993, however he continued to assist with management until 1996. He has also been vice president and manager of bank operations for Midwest Federal Savings & Loan Association, was part owner of an air transportation business that provided air and ground courier services to financial institutions, Check Flight Inc., and spent 22 years with First Bank Minneapolis in various positions.

Steven A. Rathgaber

Steven A. Rathgaber is executive vice president for NYCE Corp., operator of the NYCE Network, which was formed in 1994 when the New York Switch Corporation and New England Network Inc. merged. As executive vice president, Rathgaber is responsible for sales planning and management, client services, technology research and planning, and data center and remote service operations. Before the merger, Rathgaber was senior vice president of systems and operations for the NYCE Network. Before joining NYCE, he spent two years at

Veritas Venture Inc., where he served as product/project manager and was a founding principal of the company. Rathgaber has also served in various positions in the EFT industry. He earned his B.S. in accounting from St. John's University and has pursued a master's degree in financial management at Pace University.

Kenneth Rosenblum

Kenneth Rosenblum is a senior vice president and manager of retail distribution planning for Chase Manhattan Bank. His responsibilities include managing the branch network portfolio management, overseeing market area analysis for branch and other channel deployment decisions, developing strategy and information resources for the spectrum of distribution channels, and planning the tactical migration of customers to alternative delivery channels. Rosenblum's previous experience includes key roles in two major mergers: formulating branch network action plans for the Chase Manhattan Bank—Chemical Bank merger in 1996, and managing the development and implementation of the branch network consolidation process for the Chemical and Manufacturers Hanover Trust merger in 1992. He has a master's degree in finance from Carnegie Mellon University and a bachelor's degree in electrical engineering and urban studies from the University of Rochester.

Elisabeth Rhyne

Elisabeth Rhyne is director of the Office of Microenterprise Development at the U.S. Agency for International Development (USAID) and leads the agency's implementation of its Microenterprise Initiative. Dr. Rhyne has worked for 15 years on economic development, especially in the area of small enterprise and finance, both domestically and internationally. She has consulted on microenterprise development and financial sector reform in countries around the world and designed and managed major USAID projects and initiatives for promoting microenterprise development. Dr. Rhyne has also worked on domestic policy issues at the Office of Management and Budget, the Congressional Budget Office, and the

Brookings Institution. She is adjunct professor at the Johns Hopkins University School of Advanced International Studies and the author of numerous articles and books, including *The New World of Microenterprise Finance; Banks, Small Business and the SBA Loan Guarantee Program; and The Economics of Federal Credit Policy.* Dr. Rhyne holds a Ph.D. in public policy from Harvard University and a B.A. in history and humanities from Stanford University.

Michael Sherraden

Michael Sherraden is the Benjamin E. Youngdahl Professor of Social Development and director of the Center for Social Develoment (CSD) at Washington University in St. Louis. He is author of *Assets and the Poor: A New American Welfare Policy* and co-editor of *Alternatives to Social Security: An International Inquiry.* Professor Sherraden has proposed individual development accounts (IDAs), which are matched savings accounts for the poor, as an asset building strategy. IDAs are being adopted in a number of states and community organizations.

Larry D. Stout

Assistant Commissioner Larry D. Stout has worked for the Financial Management Service, Department of the Treasury, since 1992. The agency manages all federal cash and credit activities, and Stout is responsible for the cash flow management of more than $2 trillion annually. He began his federal career in 1966 with the U.S. General Accounting Office and has held various jobs in the financial management arena for the past 29 years. He has worked for the Treasury Department, Department of Agriculture, and the National Bureau of Standards. He was also selected for a fellowship and spent a year as a staff member for the U.S. Senate Committee on Appropriations. He has a B.S. in accounting, a M.S. in administration, and is a graduate of the Federal Executive Institute and Harvard University's Program for Senior Managers in Government. Stout is an adjunct faculty member at Northern Virginia Community College and has taught financial management in several of the former Soviet republics. He is an active member of the Washington chapter of the Association of Government Accountants (AGA) from which he received the 1990 AGA Washington Chapter Achievement of the Year Award. He also received a Presidential Rank Award in 1995 for his leadership in improving financial management in the federal government.

Thomas W. Swidarski

Thomas W. Swidarski is director of financial industry worldwide marketing for Diebold Inc., which provides card-based transaction systems, security, and service solutions to the financial, education, and health care industries. He is responsible for analyzing financial industry trends and leveraging Diebold's core competencies to ensure proper positions for future growth. Swidarski has held various positions in the financial industry, focusing on marketing, product management, profitability, branding, and retail distribution. He is a former senior vice president at PNC Bank Kentucky and more recently was responsible for consumer marketing for the entire corporation. He received a degree in marketing and management at the University of Dayton, Ohio, and a master's degree in business management from Cleveland State University.

Robert M. Townsend

Robert M. Townsend is currently Charles E. Merriam Professor of Economics in the Department of Economics and a research associate at the National Opinion Research Center (NORC) at the University of Chicago. He began to teach and research at Carnegie-Mellon University. He is a member of the Econometric Society, the American Academy of Arts and Sciences, and has served as editor of the *Journal of Political Economy* and panel member in economics for the National Science Foundation. Townsend received a B.A. from Duke University and a Ph.D. from the Unversity of Minnesota.

Douglas B. Woodruff

As president of Boatmen's Community Development Corporation, Douglas B. Woodruff is responsible for directing and implementing Community Reinvestment Act policy through the nine states in which the company operates.

He also oversees the evaluation, selection, and monitoring of the company's community development investments in its various markets. Previously, Woodruff was chief operation officer of Boatmen's Community Development Corporation and was vice president and manager of government and community relations for the Boatmen's National Bank of St. Louis. The bank has been recognized as one of the country's leading institutions in community development, having instituted numerous products and programs designed to benefit low-income areas of the community. Woodruff is also a member of the board of directors of the National Association of Affordable Housing Lenders and serves on the Consumer Bankers Association's community reinvestment committee. He is the current chairman of the St. Louis equity fund investment committee, the former chairman of the St. Louis Regional Housing Alliance, and a commissioner for the St. Louis County Housing Resource Commission. He is a graduate of Miami University, Oxford, Ohio, and the Stonier Graduate School of Banking.

Brenda Yost

Brenda Yost is senior vice president of Consumer Electronic Banking Product and Delivery Support for Bank of America. She is responsible for project management of the bank's Electronic Benefits Transfer and related services. She also supports the bank's Asia Retail Division on strategy and implementation of electronic banking and call centers. Previously Ms. Yost managed risk policies for retail electronic and liability products and directed marketing and product managment for the Consumer Electronic Banking Division. Additionally, she worked for VISA International, the Office of the Comptroller of the Currency, and the National Automated Clearinghouse Association. Ms. Yost has a master's degree in consumer economics from Ohio State University.

Forum Background Readings

Philip Bond and Robert Townsend, "Formal and Informal Financing in a Chicago Ethnic Neighborhood," Federal Reserve Bank of Chicago *Economic Perspectives*, July/August 1996.

John P. Caskey, "Consumer Financial Services and the Poor," Swarthmore College, Working Paper, October 1996. Final version published as John P. Caskey, *Lower Income Americans, Higher Cost Financial Services*. 1977. Filene Research Institute: Madison, Wisconsin.

"Hispanics Tell of Armed Robberies," *The Durham Herald-Sun*, January 8, 1997, p. C1.

Lawrence J. Radecki, John Wenninger, and Daniel K. Orlow, "Bank Branches in Supermarkets," Federal Reserve Bank of New York, *Current Issues in Economics and Finance*, Volume 2, Number 13, December 1996.

Marguerite S. Robinson, "Savings Mobilization and Microenterprise Finance: The Indonesian Experience," in Maria Otero and Elisabeth Rhyne eds., *The New World of Microenterprise Finance: Building Healthy Financial Institutions for the Poor*. 1994. Kumarian Press: West Hartford, Connecticut.